Hope you find
some inspiration
in here

B. Cunn

"Amazing. That was my first word, when I started reading this book. Fascinating was the next. Amazing, because once again, Bernard masterfully takes a complex subject, and translates it into something anyone can understand. Fascinating because the detailed real-life customer examples immediately inspired me to think about my own customers and partners, and how they could emulate the success of these companies. Bernard's book is a must have for all Big Data practitioners and Big Data hopefuls!"

**Shawn Ahmed, Senior Director, Business Analytics and IoT at Splunk**

"Finally a book that stops talking theory and starts talking facts. Providing real-life and tangible insights for practices, processes, technology and *teams* that support Big Data, across a portfolio of organizations and industries. We often think Big Data is big business and big cost, however some of the most interesting examples show how small businesses can use smart data to make a real difference. The businesses in the book illustrate how Big Data is fundamentally about the customer, and generating a data-driven customer strategy that influences both staff and customers at every touch point of the customer journey."

**Adrian Clowes, Head of Data and Analytics at Center Parcs UK**

"*Big Data in Practice* by Bernard Marr is the most complete book on the Big Data and analytics ecosystem. The many real-life examples make it equally relevant for the novice as well as experienced data scientists."

**Fouad Bendris, Business Technologist, Big Data Lead at Hewlett Packard Enterprise**

"Bernard Marr is one of the leading authors in the domain of Big Data. Throughout *Big Data in Practice* Marr generously shares some of his keen insights into the practical value delivered to a huge range of different businesses from their Big Data initiatives. This fascinating book provides excellent clues as to the secret sauce required in order to successfully deliver competitive advantage through Big Data analytics. The logical structure of the book means that it is as easy to consume in one sitting as it is to pick up from time to time. This is a must-read for any Big Data sceptics or business leaders looking for inspiration."

**Will Cashman, Head of Customer Analytics at AIB**

"The business of business is now data! Bernard Marr's book delivers concrete, valuable, and diverse insights on Big Data use cases, success stories, and lessons learned from numerous business domains. After diving into this book, you will have all the knowledge you need to crush the Big Data hype machine, to soar to new heights of data analytics ROI, and to gain competitive advantage from the data within your organization."

**Kirk Borne, Principal Data Scientist at Booz Allen Hamilton, USA**

"Big Data is disrupting every aspect of business. You're holding a book that provides powerful examples of how companies strive to defy outmoded business models and design new ones with Big Data in mind."

**Henrik von Scheel, Google Advisory Board Member**

"Bernard Marr provides a comprehensive overview of how far Big Data has come in past years. With inspiring examples he clearly shows how large, and small, organizations can benefit from Big Data. This book is a must-read for any organization that wants to be a data-driven business."

**Mark van Rijmenam, Author *Think Bigger* and Founder of Datafloq**

"This is one of those unique business books that is as useful as it is interesting. Bernard has provided us with a unique, inside look at how leading organizations are leveraging new technology to deliver real value out of data and completely transforming the way we think, work, and live."

**Stuart Frankel, CEO at Narrative Science Inc.**

"Big Data can be a confusing subject for even sophisticated data analysts. Bernard has done a fantastic job of illustrating the true business benefits of Big Data. In this book you find out succinctly how leading companies are getting real value from Big Data – highly recommended read!'

**Arthur Lee, Vice President of Qlik Analytics at Qlik**

"If you are searching for the missing link between Big Data technology and achieving business value – look no further! From the world of science to entertainment, Bernard Marr delivers it – and, importantly, shares with us the recipes for success."

**Achim Granzen, Chief Technologist Analytics at Hewlett Packard Enterprise**

"A comprehensive compendium of why, how, and to what effects Big Data analytics are used in today's world."

**James Kobielus, Big Data Evangelist at IBM**

"A treasure chest of Big Data use cases."

**Stefan Groschupf, CEO at Datameer, Inc.**

# BIG DATA IN PRACTICE

# BIG DATA IN PRACTICE

## HOW 45 SUCCESSFUL COMPANIES USED BIG DATA ANALYTICS TO DELIVER EXTRAORDINARY RESULTS

## BERNARD MARR

WILEY

This edition first published 2016

© 2016 Bernard Marr

*Registered office*
John Wiley and Sons Ltd, The Atrium, Southern Gate, Chichester, West Sussex, PO19 8SQ,
United Kingdom

For details of our global editorial offices, for customer services and for information about how to
apply for permission to reuse the copyright material in this book please see our website at
www.wiley.com.

*Library of Congress Cataloging-in-Publication Data is available*

A catalogue record for this book is available from the British Library.

ISBN 978-1-119-23138-7 (hbk)    ISBN 978-1-119-23139-4 (ebk)
ISBN 978-1-119-23141-7 (ebk)    ISBN 978-1-119-27882-5 (ebk)

Cover Design: Wiley
Cover Image: © vs148/Shutterstock

Set in 11/14pt MinionPro Light by Aptara Inc., New Delhi, India
Printed in Great Britain by TJ International Ltd, Padstow, Cornwall, UK

*This book is dedicated to the people who mean most to me: My wife Claire and our three children Sophia, James and Oliver.*

# CONTENTS

# CONTENTS

# CONTENTS

Contents

# INTRODUCTION

We are witnessing a movement that will completely transform any part of business and society. The word we have given to this movement is Big Data and it will change everything, from the way banks and shops operate to the way we treat cancer and protect our world from terrorism. No matter what job you are in and no matter what industry you work in, Big Data will transform it.

Some people believe that Big Data is just a big fad that will go away if they ignore it for long enough. It won't! The hype around Big Data and the name may disappear (which wouldn't be a great loss), but the phenomenon will stay and only gather momentum. What we call Big Data today will simply become the new normal in a few years' time, when all businesses and government organizations use large volumes of data to improve what they do and how they do it.

I work every day with companies and government organizations on Big Data projects and thought it would be a good idea to share how Big Data is used today, across lots of different industries, among big and small companies, to deliver real value. But first things first, let's just look at what Big Data actually means.

## What Is Big Data?

Big Data basically refers to the fact that we can now collect and analyse data in ways that was simply impossible even a few years ago. There are two things that are fuelling this Big Data movement: the fact we have more data on anything and our improved ability to store and analyse any data.

## More Data On Everything

Everything we do in our increasingly digitized world leaves a data trail. This means the amount of data available is literally exploding. We have created more data in the past two years than in the entire previous history of mankind. By 2020, it is predicted that about 1.7 megabytes of new data will be created every second, for every human being on the planet. This data is coming not just from the tens of millions of messages and emails we send each other every second via email, WhatsApp, Facebook, Twitter, etc. but also from the one trillion digital photos we take each year and the increasing amounts of video data we generate (every single minute we currently upload about 300 hours of new video to YouTube and we share almost three million videos on Facebook). On top of that, we have data from all the sensors we are now surrounded by. The latest smartphones have sensors to tell where we are (GPS), how fast we are moving (accelerometer), what the weather is like around us (barometer), what force we are using to press the touch screen (touch sensor) and much more. By 2020, we will have over six billion smartphones in the world – all full of sensors that collect data. But not only our phones are getting smart, we now have smart TVs, smart watches, smart meters, smart kettles, fridges, tennis rackets and even smart light bulbs. In fact, by 2020, we will have over 50 billion devices that are connected to the Internet. All this means that the amount of data and the variety of data (from sensor data, to text and video) in the world will grow to unimaginable levels.

## Ability To Analyse Everything

All this Big Data is worth very little unless we are able to turn it into insights. In order to do that we need to capture and analyse the data.

In the past, there were limitations to the amount of data that could be stored in databases – the more data there was, the slower the system became. This can now be overcome with new techniques that allow us to store and analyse data across different databases, in distributed locations, connected via networks. So-called distributed computing means huge amounts of data can be stored (in little bits across lots of databases) and analysed by sharing the analysis between different servers (each performing a small part of the analysis).

Google were instrumental in developing distributed computing technology, enabling them to search the Internet. Today, about 1000 computers are involved in answering a single search query, which takes no more than 0.2 seconds to complete. We currently search 3.5 billion times a day on Google alone.

Distributed computing tools such as Hadoop manage the storage and analysis of Big Data across connected databases and servers. What's more, Big Data storage and analysis technology is now available to rent in a software-as-a-service (SAAS) model, which makes Big Data analytics accessible to anyone, even those with low budgets and limited IT support.

Finally, we are seeing amazing advancements in the way we can analyse data. Algorithms can now look at photos, identify who is on them and then search the Internet for other pictures of that person. Algorithms can now understand spoken words, translate them into written text and analyse this text for content, meaning and sentiment (e.g. are we saying nice things or not-so-nice things?). More and more advanced algorithms emerge every day to help us understand our world and predict the future. Couple all this with machine learning and artificial intelligence (the ability of algorithms to learn and make decisions independently) and you can hopefully see that the developments and opportunities here are very exciting and evolving very quickly.

# Big Data Opportunities

With this book I wanted to showcase the current state of the art in Big Data and provide an overview of how companies and organizations across all different industries are using Big Data to deliver value in diverse areas. You will see I have covered areas including how retailers (both traditional bricks 'n' mortar companies as well as online ones) use Big Data to predict trends and consumer behaviours, how governments are using Big Data to foil terrorist plots, even how a tiny family butcher or a zoo use Big Data to improve performance, as well as the use of Big Data in cities, telecoms, sports, gambling, fashion, manufacturing, research, motor racing, video gaming and everything in between.

Instead of putting their heads in the sand or getting lost in this startling new world of Big Data, the companies I have featured here have figured out smart ways to use data in order to deliver strategic value. In my previous book, *Big Data: Using SMART Big Data, Analytics and Metrics to Make Better Decisions and Improve Performance* (also published by Wiley), I go into more detail on how any company can figure out how to use Big Data to deliver value.

I am convinced that Big Data, unlike any other trend at the moment, will affect everyone and everything we do. You can read this book cover to cover for a complete overview of current Big Data use cases or you can use it as a reference book and dive in and out of the areas you find most interesting or are relevant to you or your clients. I hope you enjoy it!

# 1
# WALMART

*How Big Data Is Used To Drive Supermarket Performance*

## Background

Walmart are the largest retailer in the world and the world's largest company by revenue, with over two million employees and 20,000 stores in 28 countries.

With operations on this scale it's no surprise that they have long seen the value in data analytics. In 2004, when Hurricane Sandy hit the US, they found that unexpected insights could come to light when data was studied as a whole, rather than as isolated individual sets. Attempting to forecast demand for emergency supplies in the face of the approaching Hurricane Sandy, CIO Linda Dillman turned up some surprising statistics. As well as flashlights and emergency equipment, expected bad weather had led to an upsurge in sales of strawberry Pop Tarts in several other locations. Extra supplies of these were dispatched to stores in Hurricane Frances's path in 2012, and sold extremely well.

Walmart have grown their Big Data and analytics department considerably since then, continuously staying on the cutting edge. In 2015, the company announced they were in the process of creating the world's largest private data cloud, to enable the processing of 2.5 petabytes of information every hour.

## What Problem Is Big Data Helping To Solve?

Supermarkets sell millions of products to millions of people every day. It's a fiercely competitive industry which a large proportion of people living in the developed world count on to provide them with day-to-day essentials. Supermarkets compete not just on price but also on customer service and, vitally, convenience. Having the right products in the right place at the right time, so the right people can buy them, presents huge logistical problems. Products have to be efficiently priced to the cent, to stay competitive. And if customers find they can't get everything they need under one roof, they will look elsewhere for somewhere to shop that is a better fit for their busy schedule.

## How Is Big Data Used In Practice?

In 2011, with a growing awareness of how data could be used to understand their customers' needs and provide them with the products they wanted to buy, Walmart established @WalmartLabs and their Fast Big Data Team to research and deploy new data-led initiatives across the business.

The culmination of this strategy was referred to as the Data Café – a state-of-the-art analytics hub at their Bentonville, Arkansas headquarters. At the Café, the analytics team can monitor 200 streams of internal and external data in real time, including a 40-petabyte database of all the sales transactions in the previous weeks.

Timely analysis of real-time data is seen as key to driving business performance – as Walmart Senior Statistical Analyst Naveen Peddamail tells me: "If you can't get insights until you've analysed your sales for a week or a month, then you've lost sales within that time.

"Our goal is always to get information to our business partners as fast as we can, so they can take action and cut down the turnaround time. It is proactive and reactive analytics."

Teams from any part of the business are invited to visit the Café with their data problems, and work with the analysts to devise a solution. There is also a system which monitors performance indicators across the company and triggers automated alerts when they hit a certain level – inviting the teams responsible for them to talk to the data team about possible solutions.

Peddamail gives an example of a grocery team struggling to understand why sales of a particular produce were unexpectedly declining. Once their data was in the hands of the Café analysts, it was established very quickly that the decline was directly attributable to a pricing error. The error was immediately rectified and sales recovered within days.

Sales across different stores in different geographical areas can also be monitored in real-time. One Halloween, Peddamail recalls, sales figures of novelty cookies were being monitored, when analysts saw that there were several locations where they weren't selling at all. This enabled them to trigger an alert to the merchandising teams responsible for those stores, who quickly realized that the products hadn't even been put on the shelves. Not exactly a complex algorithm, but it wouldn't have been possible without real-time analytics.

Another initiative is Walmart's Social Genome Project, which monitors public social media conversations and attempts to predict what products people will buy based on their conversations. They also have the Shopycat service, which predicts how people's shopping habits are influenced by their friends (using social media data again) and have developed their own search engine, named Polaris, to allow them to analyse search terms entered by customers on their websites.

## What Were The Results?

Walmart tell me that the Data Café system has led to a reduction in the time it takes from a problem being spotted in the numbers to a solution being proposed from an average of two to three weeks down to around 20 minutes.

## What Data Was Used?

The Data Café uses a constantly refreshed database consisting of 200 billion rows of transactional data – and that only represents the most recent few weeks of business!

On top of that it pulls in data from 200 other sources, including meteorological data, economic data, telecoms data, social media data, gas prices and a database of events taking place in the vicinity of Walmart stores.

## What Are The Technical Details?

Walmart's real-time transactional database consists of 40 petabytes of data. Huge though this volume of transactional data is, it only includes from the most recent weeks' data, as this is where the value, as far as real-time analysis goes, is to be found. Data from across the chain's stores, online divisions and corporate units are stored centrally on Hadoop (a distributed data storage and data management system).

CTO Jeremy King has described the approach as "data democracy" as the aim is to make it available to anyone in the business who can make use of it. At some point after the adoption of distributed Hadoop framework in 2011, analysts became concerned that the volume was growing at a rate that could hamper their ability to analyse it. As a result, a policy of "intelligently managing" data collection was adopted which involved setting up several systems designed to refine and categorize the data before it was stored. Other technologies in use include Spark and Cassandra, and languages including R and SAS are used to develop analytical applications.

## Any Challenges That Had To Be Overcome?

With an analytics operation as ambitious as the one planned by Walmart, the rapid expansion required a large intake of new staff, and finding the right people with the right skills proved difficult. This problem is far from restricted to Walmart: a recent survey by researchers Gartner found that more than half of businesses feel their ability to carry out Big Data analytics is hampered by difficulty in hiring the appropriate talent.

One of the approaches Walmart took to solving this was to turn to crowdsourced data science competition website Kaggle – which I profile in Chapter 44.[1]

Kaggle set users of the website a challenge involving predicting how promotional and seasonal events such as stock-clearance sales and holidays would influence sales of a number of different products. Those who came up with models that most closely matched the real-life data gathered by Walmart were invited to apply for positions on the data science team. In fact, one of those who found himself working for Walmart after taking part in the competition was Naveen Peddamail, whose thoughts I have included in this chapter.

Once a new analyst starts at Walmart, they are put through their Analytics Rotation Program. This sees them moved through each different team with responsibility for analytical work, to allow them to gain a broad overview of how analytics is used across the business.

Walmart's senior recruiter for its Information Systems Operation, Mandar Thakur, told me: "The Kaggle competition created a buzz about Walmart and our analytics organization. People always knew that Walmart generates and has a lot of data, but the best part was that this let people see how we are using it strategically."

## What Are The Key Learning Points And Takeaways?

Supermarkets are big, fast, constantly changing businesses that are complex organisms consisting of many individual subsystems. This makes them an ideal business in which to apply Big Data analytics.

Success in business is driven by competition. Walmart have always taken a lead in data-driven initiatives, such as loyalty and reward programmes, and by wholeheartedly committing themselves to the latest advances in real-time, responsive analytics they have shown they plan to remain competitive.

Bricks 'n' mortar retail may be seen as "low tech" – almost Stone Age, in fact – compared to their flashy, online rivals but Walmart have shown that cutting-edge Big Data is just as relevant to them as it is to Amazon or Alibaba.[2] Despite the seemingly more convenient options on offer, it appears that customers, whether through habit or preference, are still willing to get in their cars and travel to shops to buy things in person. This means there is still a huge market out there for the taking, and businesses that make best use of analytics in order to drive efficiency and improve their customers' experience are set to prosper.

### REFERENCES AND FURTHER READING

1. Kaggle (2015) Predict how sales of weather-sensitive products are affected by snow and rain, https://www.kaggle.com/c/walmart-recruiting-sales-in-stormy-weather, accessed 5 January 2016.
2. Walmart (2015) When data met retail: A #lovedata story, http://careersblog.walmart.com/when-data-met-retail-a-lovedata-story/, accessed 5 January 2016.

# 2
# CERN

## *Unravelling The Secrets Of The Universe With Big Data*

## Background

CERN are the international scientific research organization that operate the Large Hadron Collider (LHC), humanity's biggest and most advanced physics experiment. The colliders, encased in 17 miles of tunnels buried 600 feet below the surface of Switzerland and France, aim to simulate conditions in the universe milliseconds following the Big Bang. This allows physicists to search for elusive theoretical particles, such as the Higgs boson, which could give us unprecedented insight into the composition of the universe.

CERN's projects, such as the LHC, would not be possible if it weren't for the Internet and Big Data – in fact, the Internet was originally created at CERN in the 1990s. Tim Berners-Lee, the man often referred to as the "father of the Internet", developed the hypertext protocol which holds together the World Wide Web while at CERN. Its original purpose was to facilitate communication between researchers around the globe.

The LHC alone generates around 30 petabytes of information per year – 15 trillion pages of printed text, enough to fill 600 million filling cabinets – clearly Big Data by anyone's standards!

In 2013, CERN announced that the Higgs boson had been found. Many scientists have taken this as proof that the standard model of particle physics is correct. This confirms that much of what we think we know about the workings of the universe on a subatomic level is essentially right, although there are still many mysteries remaining, particularly involving gravity and dark matter.

## What Problem Is Big Data Helping To Solve?

The collisions monitored in the LHC happen very quickly, and the resulting subatomic "debris" containing the elusive, sought-after particles exists for only a few millionths of a second before they decay. The exact conditions that cause the release of the particles which CERN are looking for only occur under very precise conditions, and as a result many hundreds of millions of collisions have to be monitored and recorded every second in the hope that the sensors will pick them up.

The LHC's sensors record hundreds of millions of collisions between particles, some of which achieve speeds of just a fraction under the speed of light as they are accelerated around the collider. This generates a massive amount of data and requires very sensitive and precise equipment to measure and record the results.

## How Is Big Data Used In Practice?

The LHC is used in four main experiments, involving around 8000 analysts across the globe. They use the data to search for elusive theoretical particles and probe for the answers to questions involving antimatter, dark matter and extra dimensions in time and space.

Data is collected by sensors inside the collider that monitor hundreds of millions of particle collisions every second. The sensors pick up light, so they are essentially cameras, with a 100-megapixel resolution capable of capturing images at incredibly high speeds.

This data is then analysed by algorithms that are tuned to pick up the telltale energy signatures left behind by the appearance and disappearance of the exotic particles CERN are searching for.

The algorithms compare the resulting images with theoretical data explaining how we believe the target particles, such as the Higgs boson, will act. If the results match, it is evidence the sensors have found the target particles.

## What Were The Results?

In 2013, CERN scientists announced that they believed they had observed and recorded the existence of the Higgs boson. This was a huge leap forward for science as the existence of the particle had been theorized for decades but could not be proven until technology was developed on this scale.

The discovery has given scientists unprecedented insight into the fundamental structure of the universe and the complex relationships between the fundamental particles that everything we see, experience and interact with is built from.

Apart from the LHC, CERN has existed since the 1950s and has been responsible for a great many scientific breakthroughs with earlier experiments, and many world-leading scientists have made their name through their work with the organization.

## What Data Was Used?

Primarily, the LHC gathers data using light sensors to record the collision, and fallout, from protons accelerated to 99.9% of the speed of light. Sensors inside the colliders pick up light energy emitted during the collisions and from the decay of the resulting particles, and convert it into data which can be analysed by computer algorithms.

Much of this data, being essentially photographs, is unstructured. Algorithms transform light patterns recorded by the sensors into mathematical data. Theoretical data – ideas about how we think the particles being hunted will act – is matched against the sensor data to determine what has been captured on camera.

## What Are The Technical Details?

The Worldwide LHC Computing Grid is the world's largest distributed computing network, spanning 170 computing centres in 35 different countries. To develop distributed systems capable of analysing 30 petabytes of information per year, CERN instigated the openlab project, in collaboration with data experts at companies including Oracle, Intel and Siemens. The network consists of over 200,000 cores and 15 petabytes of disk space.

The 300 gigabytes per second of data provided by the seven CERN sensors is eventually whittled down to 300 megabytes per second of "useful" data, which constitutes the product's raw output. This data is made available as a real-time stream to academic institutions partnered with CERN.

CERN have developed methods of adding extra computing power on the fly to increase the processing output of the grid without taking it offline, in times of spikes in demand for computational power.

## Any Challenges That Had To Be Overcome?

The LHC gathers incredibly vast amounts of data, very quickly. No organization on earth has the computing power and resources necessary to analyse that data in a timely fashion. To deal with this, CERN turned to distributed computing.

They had already been using distributed computed for some time. In fact, the Internet as we know it today was initially built to save scientists from having to travel to Geneva whenever they wanted to analyse results of CERN's earlier experiments.

For the LHC, CERN created the LHC Distributed Computing Grid, which comprises 170 computer centres in 35 countries. Many of these are private computing centres operated by the academic and commercial organizations partnered with CERN.

This parallel, distributed use of computer processing power means far more calculations per second can be carried out than even the world's most powerful supercomputers could manage alone.

## What Are The Key Learning Points And Takeaways?

The groundbreaking work carried out by CERN, which has greatly improved our knowledge of how the universe works, would not be possible without Big Data and analytics.

CERN and Big Data have evolved together: CERN was one of the primary catalysts in the development of the Internet which brought about the Big Data age we live in today.

Distributed computing makes it possible to carry out tasks that are far beyond the capabilities of any one organization to complete alone.

### REFERENCES AND FURTHER READING

Purcell, A. (2013) CERN on preparing for tomorrow's big data, http://home.web.cern.ch/about/updates/2013/10/preparing-tomorrows-big-data

Darrow, B. (2013) Attacking CERN's big data problem, https://gigaom.com/2013/09/18/attacking-cerns-big-data-problem/

O'Luanaigh, C. (2013) Exploration on the big data frontier, http://home.web.cern.ch/students-educators/updates/2013/05/exploration-big-data-frontier

Smith, T. (2015) Video on CERN's big data, https://www.youtube.com/watch?v=j-0cUmUyb-Y

# 3
# NETFLIX

*How Netflix Used Big Data To Give Us The*
*Programmes We Want*

## Background

The streaming movie and TV service Netflix are said to account for one-third of peak-time Internet traffic in the US, and the service now have 65 million members in over 50 countries enjoying more than 100 million hours of TV shows and movies a day. Data from these millions of subscribers is collected and monitored in an attempt to understand our viewing habits. But Netflix's data isn't just "big" in the literal sense. It is the combination of this data with cutting-edge analytical techniques that makes Netflix a true Big Data company.

## What Problem Is Big Data Helping To Solve?

Legendary Hollywood screenwriter William Goldman said: "Nobody, nobody – not now, not ever – knows the least goddam thing about what is or isn't going to work at the box office."

He was speaking before the arrival of the Internet and Big Data and, since then, Netflix have been determined to prove him wrong by building a business around predicting exactly what we'll enjoy watching.

# How Is Big Data Used In Practice?

A quick glance at Netflix's jobs page is enough to give you an idea of how seriously data and analytics are taken. Specialists are recruited to join teams specifically skilled in applying analytical skills to particular business areas: personalization analytics, messaging analytics, content delivery analytics, device analytics … the list goes on. However, although Big Data is used across every aspect of the Netflix business, their holy grail has always been to predict what customers will enjoy watching. Big Data analytics is the fuel that fires the "recommendation engines" designed to serve this purpose.

Efforts here began back in 2006, when the company were still primarily a DVD-mailing business (streaming began a year later). They launched the Netflix Prize, offering $1 million to the group that could come up with the best algorithm for predicting how their customers would rate a movie based on their previous ratings. The winning entry was finally announced in 2009 and, although the algorithms are constantly revised and added to, the principles are still a key element of the recommendation engine.

At first, analysts were limited by the lack of information they had on their customers – only four data points (customer ID, movie ID, rating and the date the movie was watched) were available for analysis. As soon as streaming became the primary delivery method, many new data points on their customers became accessible. This new data enabled Netflix to build models to predict the perfect storm situation of customers consistently being served with movies they would enjoy. Happy customers, after all, are far more likely to continue their subscriptions.

Another central element to Netflix's attempt to give us films we will enjoy is tagging. The company pay people to watch movies and then tag them with elements the movies contain. They will then suggest you watch other productions that were tagged similarly to those you enjoyed. This is where the sometimes unusual (and slightly robotic-sounding) "suggestions" come from: "In the mood for wacky teen comedy featuring a strong female lead?" It's also the reason the service will sometimes (in fact, in my experience, often!) recommend I watch films that have been rated with only one or two stars. This may seem counterintuitive to their objective of showing me films I will enjoy. But what has happened is that the weighting of these ratings has been outweighed by the prediction that the content of the movie will appeal. In fact, Netflix have effectively defined nearly 80,000 new "micro-genres" of movie based on our viewing habits!

More recently, Netflix have moved towards positioning themselves as a content creator, not just a distribution method for movie studios and other networks. Their strategy here has also been firmly driven by their data – which showed that their subscribers had a voracious appetite for content directed by David Fincher and starring Kevin Spacey. After outbidding networks including HBO and ABC for the rights to *House of Cards*, they were so confident it fitted their predictive model for the "perfect TV show" that they bucked the convention of producing a pilot and immediately commissioned two seasons comprising 26 episodes. Every aspect of the production under the control of Netflix was informed by data – even the range of colours used on the cover image for the series was selected to draw viewers in.

The ultimate metric Netflix hope to improve is the number of hours customers spend using their service. You don't really need statistics to tell you that viewers who don't spend much time using the service are likely to feel they aren't getting value for money from their subscriptions, and so may cancel their subscriptions. To this end, the way various factors affect the "quality of experience" is closely monitored and models are built to explore how this affects user behaviour. By collecting end-user data on how the physical location of the content affects the viewer's experience, calculations about the placement of data can be made to ensure there is an optimal service to as many homes as possible.

## What Were The Results?

Netflix's letter to shareholders in April 2015 shows their Big Data strategy was paying off. They added 4.9 million new subscribers in Q1 2015, compared to four million in the same period in 2014. Netflix put much of this success down to their "ever-improving content", including *House of Cards* and *Orange is the New Black*. This original content is driving new member acquisition and customer retention. In fact, 90% of Netflix members have engaged with this original content. Obviously, their ability to predict what viewers will enjoy is a large part of this success.

And what about their ultimate metric: how many hours customers spend using the service? Well, in Q1 2015 alone, Netflix members streamed 10 billion hours of content. If Netflix's Big Data strategy continues to evolve, that number is set to increase.

## What Data Was Used?

The recommendation algorithms and content decisions are fed by data on what titles customers watch, what time of day movies are watched, time spent selecting movies, how often playback is stopped (either by the user or owing to network limitations) and ratings given. In order to analyse quality of experience, Netflix collect data on delays caused by buffering (rebuffer rate) and bitrate (which affects the picture quality), as well as customer location.

## What Are The Technical Details?

Although their vast catalogue of movies and TV shows is hosted in the cloud on Amazon Web Services (AWS), it is also mirrored around the world by ISPs and other hosts. As well as improving user experience by reducing lag when streaming content around the globe, this reduces costs for the ISPs – saving them from the cost of downloading the data from the Netflix server before passing it on to the viewers at home.

In 2013, the size of their catalogue was said to exceed three petabytes. This humungous amount of data is accounted for by the need to hold many of their titles in up to 120 different video formats, owing to the number of different devices offering Netflix playback.

Originally, their systems used Oracle databases, but they switched to NoSQL and Cassandra to allow more complex, Big Data-driven analysis of unstructured data.

Speaking at the Strata + Hadoop World conference, Kurt Brown, who leads the Data Platform team at Netflix, explained how Netflix's data platform is constantly evolving. The Netflix data infrastructure includes Big Data technologies like Hadoop, Hive and Pig plus traditional business intelligence tools like Teradata and MicroStrategy. It also includes Netflix's own open-source applications and services Lipstick and Genie. And, like all of Netflix's core infrastructure, it all runs in the AWS cloud. Going forward, Netflix are exploring Spark for streaming, machine learning and analytic use cases, and they're continuing to develop new additions for their own open-source suite.

## Any Challenges That Had To Be Overcome?

Although a lot of the metadata collected by Netflix – which actors a viewer likes to watch and what time of day they watch films or TV – is simple, easily quantified structured data, Netflix realized early on that a lot of valuable data is also stored in the messy, unstructured content of video and audio.

To make this data available for computer analysis and therefore unlock its value, it had to be quantified in some way. Netflix did this by paying teams of viewers, numbering in their thousands, to sit through hours of content, meticulously tagging elements they found in them.

After reading a 32-page handbook, these paid viewers marked up themes, issues and motifs that took place on screen, such as a hero experiencing a religious epiphany or a strong female character making a tough moral choice. From this data, Netflix have identified nearly 80,000 "micro-genres" such as "comedy films featuring talking animals" or "historical dramas with gay or lesbian themes". Netflix can now identify what films you like watching far more accurately than simply seeing that you like horror films or spy films, and can use this to predict what you will want to watch. This gives the unstructured, messy data the outline of a structure that can be assessed quantitatively – one of the fundamental principles of Big Data.

Today, Netflix are said to have begun automating this process, by creating routines that can take a snapshot of the content in Jpeg format and analyse what is happening on screen using sophisticated technologies such as facial recognition and colour analysis. These snapshots can be taken either at scheduled intervals or when a user takes a particular action such as pausing or stopping playback. For example, if it knows a user fits the profile of tending to switch off after watching gory or sexual scenes, it can suggest more sedate alternatives next time they sit down to watch something.

## What Are The Key Learning Points And Takeaways?

Predicting what viewers will want to watch next is big business for networks, distributors and producers (all roles that Netflix now fill in the media industry). Netflix have taken the lead but competing services such as Hulu and Amazon Instant Box Office and, soon, Apple, can also be counted on to be improving and refining their own analytics. Predictive content programing is a field in which we can expect to see continued innovation, driven by fierce competition, as time goes on.

Netflix have begun to build the foundations of "personalized TV", where individual viewers will have their own schedule of entertainment to consume, based on analysis of their preferences. This idea has been talked about for a long time by TV networks but now we are beginning to see it become a reality in the age of Big Data.

## REFERENCES AND FURTHER READING

For more on Netflix's Big Data adventure, check out:

http://techblog.netflix.com/

http://www.netflixprize.com/http://techblog.netflix.com/2012/04/netflix-recommendations-beyond-5-stars.html

http://www.theatlantic.com/technology/archive/2014/01/how-netflix-reverse-engineered-hollywood/282679/

http://www.wired.com/insights/2014/03/big-data-lessons-netflix/

http://files.shareholder.com/downloads/NFLX/47469957x0x821407/DB785B50-90FE-44DA-9F5B-37DBF0DCD0E1/Q1_15_Earnings_Letter_final_tables.pdf

# 4
# ROLLS-ROYCE

## How Big Data Is Used To Drive Success In Manufacturing

## Background

Rolls-Royce manufacture enormous engines that are used by 500 airlines and more than 150 armed forces. These engines generate huge amounts of power, and it's no surprise that a company used to dealing with big numbers have wholeheartedly embraced Big Data.

## What Problem Is Big Data Helping To Solve?

This is an extremely high-tech industry where failures and mistakes can cost billions – and human lives. It's therefore crucial the company are able to monitor the health of their products to spot potential problems before they occur. The data Rolls-Royce gather helps them design more robust products, maintain products efficiently and provide a better service to clients.

## How Is Big Data Used In Practice?

Rolls-Royce put Big Data processes to use in three key areas of their operations: design, manufacture and after-sales support. Let's look at each area in turn.

Paul Stein, the company's chief scientific officer, says: "We have huge clusters of high-power computing which are used in the design process. We generate tens of terabytes of data on each simulation of one of our jet engines. We then have to use some pretty sophisticated computer techniques to look into that massive dataset and visualize whether that particular product we've designed is good or bad. Visualizing Big Data is just as important as the techniques we use for manipulating it." In fact, they eventually hope to be able to visualize their products in operation in all the potential extremes of behaviour in which they get used. They're already working towards this aspiration.

The company's manufacturing systems are increasingly becoming networked and communicate with each other in the drive towards a networked, Internet of Things (IoT) industrial environment. "We've just opened two world-class factories in the UK, in Rotherham and Sunderland, making discs for jet engines and turbine blades," says Stein. "The innovation is not just in the metal bashing processes, which are very sophisticated and very clever, but also in the automated measurement schemes and the way we monitor our quality control of the components we make in those factories. We are moving very rapidly towards an Internet of Things-based solution."

In terms of after-sales support, Rolls-Royce engines and propulsion systems are all fitted with hundreds of sensors that record every tiny detail about their operation and report any changes in data in real time to engineers, who then decide the best course of action. Rolls-Royce have operational service centres around the world in which expert engineers analyse the data being fed back from their engines. They can amalgamate the data from their engines to highlight factors and conditions under which engines may need maintenance. In some situations, humans will then intervene to avoid or mitigate whatever is likely to cause a problem. Increasingly, Rolls-Royce expect that computers will carry out the intervention themselves.

With civil aero engines as reliable as they are, the emphasis shifts to keeping them performing to their maximum, saving airlines fuel and meeting their schedules. Big Data analytics help Rolls-Royce identify maintenance actions days or weeks ahead of time, so airlines can schedule the work without passengers experiencing any disruption. To support this, analytics on board the engines crunch through large volumes of data generated each flight, and transmit just the pertinent highlights to the ground for further analysis. Once at the gate, the whole flight data is available for engineers to examine and detect the fine margins of performance improvement. "Data analytics are run across all of those datasets," says Stein. "We are looking for anomalies – whether pressure, temperatures or vibration measurements [which] are an indicator that an engine needs to be serviced." The huge amount of factors taken into consideration mean that when something goes wrong everything which contributed can be identified and the system can learn to predict when and where the problem is likely to repeat itself. Completing the circle, this information feeds back into the design process.

## What Were The Results?

Ultimately, Big Data analytics have helped Rolls-Royce improve the design process, decrease product development time and improve the quality and performance of their products. And, although they don't give precise figures, the company say that adopting this Big Data-driven approach to diagnosing faults, correcting them and preventing them from occurring again has "significantly" reduced costs. They also say they have streamlined production processes by allowing faults to be eliminated from future products during the design process.

It has also resulted in a new business model for the company. Obtaining this level of insight into the operation of their products means that Rolls-Royce have been able to offer a new service model to clients, which they call Total Care, where customers are charged per hour for the use of their engines, with all of the servicing costs underwritten by Rolls-Royce. "That innovation in service delivery was a game-changer, and we are very proud to have led that particular move in the industry" says Stein. "Outside of retail, it's one of the most sophisticated uses of Big Data I'm aware of."

## What Data Was Used?

At Rolls-Royce, the emphasis is most definitely on internal data, particularly sensors fitted to the company's products. Operators' data is received in the form of wireless transmissions from the aircraft (VHF radio and SATCOM en route and 3G/Wi-Fi at the gate) and contains a mixture of performance reports. These typically include snapshots of engine performance at key flight phases like take-off, where the engine is at maximum power, climb and cruise (steady state). Other reports provide detail of any interesting events during flight where high-frequency recordings pre- and post-event are available. Airplane-generated maintenance messages, movement reports (timestamps and locations) and whole-flight profiles provide even more detail.

The company are also generating a huge amount of data in their own manufacturing process. Stein gives one specific example: "At our new factory in Singapore we are generating half a terabyte of manufacturing data on each individual fan blade. We produce 6000 fan blades a year there, so that's three petabytes of data on manufacturing just one component. It's a lot of data."

## What Are The Technical Details?

### Storage

Data volumes are increasing fast, both with the growth in fleet and the increasing introduction of more data-equipped aircraft. The newest generation of engines transmits a thousand times more information than engines introduced in the 1990s. That creates a demand for low-cost, scalable storage as well as rapid processing and retrieval. Rolls-Royce maintain a robust and secure private cloud facility with a proprietary storage approach that optimizes processing throughput while maintaining a data lake for offline investigations. Looking ahead, more and more use will be made of cloud storage as more data sources are combined, including data from the IoT, opening up new services for the company's customers. This will increase the ability to mine the data to both investigate fleet performance and identify new opportunities to further improve or extend the services provided.

## Analytics

Rolls-Royce use sophisticated and class-leading data analytics to closely monitor the incoming data streams. This detects both recognized degradation modes by signature matching and novel anomalous behaviours. The emphasis on both approaches is to detect as early as possible with a confident diagnosis and prognosis, while minimizing the rate of false-positives. This is at the heart of any analytics programme, whether on big or small data – if the output either has low credibility or is not available in a timely fashion to the right people, the effort is wasted.

# Any Challenges That Had To Be Overcome?

Lack of trained and experienced data analytics staff is an often-cited challenge, and Rolls-Royce are no exception. "Skills are always an issue," says Stein. "Getting top-class talent is never easy, but you can make it easier on yourself by going where the top talent is."

To tackle this, in 2013, Rolls-Royce made Big Data research a focus of the study of their corporate lab, established in partnership with the Singapore Nanyang Technology University. Key areas of research were said to be into electrical power and control systems, manufacturing and repair technology, and computational engineering. This builds on the company's existing partnerships with top universities in the

UK and around the world, and helps ensure easier access to exciting new talent.

## What Are The Key Learning Points And Takeaways?

Rolls-Royce serve as a great example of an industrial giant of the "old age" – when innovation was about forging the future through steel and sweat – transitioning to the new age of data-enabled improvement and efficiency. As Stein puts it: "Rolls-Royce, like many successful industrials, is having to become more and more digitally aware. The digitization of Rolls-Royce is not up for debate; the question is not whether it will happen but how fast it will happen. I think of Big Data as the encroachment of digital technology into what historically have been mechanical or electronic industries. It forms a big part of our present but is going to form an even bigger part of our future."

The same applies to companies of all shapes and sizes, industrial giant or not. It's not a question of whether businesses should be using Big Data but when and how they should be using it.

### REFERENCES AND FURTHER READING

Find out more about Rolls-Royce's approach to engine health management at:

> http://www.rolls-royce.com/about/our-technology/enabling-technologies/engine-health-management.aspx#sense

# 5

# SHELL

## How Big Oil Uses Big Data

## Background

Royal Dutch Shell are the fourth-largest company in the world by revenue. Along with BP, ExxonMobil, Total and Chevron, they are one of the "supermajors" that extract most of the fuel that supplies our civilization with power.

They are a vertically integrated business, with a stake in every step of the process of transforming fossil fuel into energy for homes, vehicles and businesses – extraction, refining, packaging, distribution and retail.

In recent years, they have developed the concept of the data-driven oilfield, in an attempt to drive efficiency, reduce costs and improve safety across the industry.

## What Problem Is Big Data Helping To Solve?

The world is facing an energy crisis in the face of a growing population and ever-diminishing non-renewable resources. While attempts are being made to generate more energy from renewable or alternative sources, the vast majority of the energy we consume still comes from non-renewable oil, gas and coal.

The supply of known resources is dwindling, and the uneasy state of international politics in many areas of the world adds to the difficulty of exploration. This means the cost of extraction will inevitably rise as drillers are forced to look deeper and further afield.

The search for hydrocarbons involves huge amounts of manpower, equipment and energy. With the cost of drilling a typical deep-water oil well running to $100 million or more, it's absolutely essential drilling takes place in the locations that will provide the best rewards.

## How Is Big Data Used In Practice?

Traditionally, exploration for new resources has involved inserting sensors into the earth to pick up the low-frequency seismic waves caused by tectonic activity.

These waves of energy travelling through the earth's crust will register differently on the sensors, depending on whether they are travelling through solid rock, liquids or gaseous material, indicating the likely location of hydrocarbon deposits.

In the past, this could often prove hit and miss, however, and expensive, time-consuming exploratory drills would be needed to confirm the findings of the initial survey. In many cases, these test drills could yield disappointing results, with the cost exceeding the income that the deposits could generate.

However, thanks to our hugely increased capacity to monitor, record and analyse data, far more efficient technologies have been developed in recent years. Whereas previously a survey might have involved a few thousand readings being taken, today it will typically involve over a million. This data is then uploaded to analytics systems and compared with data from other drilling sites around the world. The more closely it matches the profiles of other sites where abundant resources have been found, the higher the probability that a full-scale drilling operation will pay off.

In addition, Big Data is also used at Shell to monitor the performance and condition of their equipment. Using techniques pioneered in the manufacturing and engineering industries, sensors collect data on the operation of each piece of equipment at a drilling site, allowing accurate forecasts to be made about its performance and likelihood of breaking down. This allows routine maintenance to be carried out more efficiently, further lowering overheads.

Across its logistics, distribution and retail functions, Big Data is amalgamated from many external sources, including local economic factors and meteorological data, which go into complex algorithms designed to determine the price we end up paying at the pumps.

## What Were The Results?

Although Shell, along with other oil and gas exploration and drilling companies, are secretive about the exact nature of the analytics they employ, and the specific data they collect, they say they are more confident than ever about their ability to forecast reserves, thanks to advanced Big Data analytics.

There's certainly a lot at stake: by increasing the amount of oil they drill around the world by just one per cent in a year, the supermajors generate enough fuel to provide the planet with power for an additional three years.

## What Data Was Used?

Shell collect data which allows them to calculate the probable size of oil and gas resources by monitoring seismic waves below the surface of the earth. The exact nature of these measurements and of the analytics is a closely guarded commercial secret, however, beyond the fact that "many millions" of these measurements are taken at any proposed site before drilling begins.

## What Are The Technical Details?

Shell use fibre-optic cables and sensor technology developed by Hewlett-Packard to carry out their surveys of potential drilling sites. The data is stored and analysed using Hadoop infrastructure running on Amazon Web Service servers. Data volumes are also an industry secret, although it is known that the first test of the system collected around one petabyte of information, and it's estimated that so far Shell have generated around 46 petabytes through their data-driven oilfield programme. Their dedicated analytics team are thought to consist of around 70 staff.

Shell are also known to have worked with IBM and movie special effects experts at DreamWorks to produce their visualization tools that give analysts 3D and 4D representations allowing them to explore forecasted reserves.

## Any Challenges That Had To Be Overcome?

The huge increase in the amount of data being generated at oil fields means that increasingly advanced analytics must be developed in order to more efficiently determine valuable signals amongst the background "noise" of the data. Large-scale system upgrades were needed as existing analytics platforms were not capable of carrying out the predictive analytics necessary to accurately make forecasts from the Big Data being generated.

In addition, there was initially resistance in the industry from some quarters to moving from a deterministic, observation-based approach to a statistically driven, probabilistic model.

Of course, much has been said recently about the potential for what are termed "unconventional resources" – such as shale gas and tight oil – to fill the gap caused by increasingly expensive conventional resources. One problem here, however, is that there is comparatively very little historical data on new and controversial methods of extracting these resources, such as fracking. However, as an arm of the industry which came into being during the Big Data revolution, this is an area of much research where rapid advances are being made.

## What Are The Key Learning Points And Takeaways?

Until science and society evolve to the point where we have reliable alternatives, the world is dependent on fossil fuel. With the difficulty of finding new reserves rising along with the cost of extraction, Big Data holds the key to driving efficiency and reducing costs of extraction and distribution.

In heavily vertically integrated industries such as fuel, efficiencies have a cumulative effect as the savings are passed along the supply chain. This means analytics can be applied to every stage of the process, identifying where bottlenecks are causing problems and efficiencies are most likely.

Although oil and gas companies consistently make huge profits, rises and falls in the cost of energy production often cause volatility in international markets and can have huge knock-on effects on our individual cost of living, as well as political ramifications. More accurate forecasting, as well as more efficient and streamlined distribution, helps to minimize this volatility.

### REFERENCES AND FURTHER READING
SAS White Paper on addressing challenges in the oil and gas industry with Big Data is available at:

> http://www.sas.com/content/dam/SAS/en_us/doc/whitepaper1/
> analytic-innovations-address-new-challenges-oil-gas-industry-
> 105974.pdf

> http://blogs.wsj.com/cio/2012/11/23/shell-is-in-a-technology-race/

# 6
# APIXIO

*How Big Data Is Transforming Healthcare*

## Background

California-based cognitive computing firm Apixio were founded in 2009 with the vision of uncovering and making accessible clinical knowledge from digitized medical records, in order to improve healthcare decision making. With their team of healthcare experts, data scientists, engineers and product experts, the company have now set their sights on enabling healthcare providers to learn from *practice*-based evidence to individually tailor care.

## What Problem Is Big Data Helping To Solve?

A staggering 80% of medical and clinical information about patients is formed of unstructured data, such as written physician notes. As Apixio CEO Darren Schulte explains, "If we want to learn how to better care for individuals and understand more about the health of the population as a whole, we need to be able to mine unstructured data for insights." Thus, the problem in healthcare is not lack of data, but the unstructured nature of its data: the many, many different formats and templates that healthcare providers use, and the numerous different systems that house this information. To tackle this problem,

Apixio devised a way to access and make sense of that clinical information.

## How Is Big Data Used In Practice?

Electronic health records (EHRs) have been around for a while, but they are not designed to facilitate data analysis and contain data stored across a number of different systems and formats. So before Apixio can even analyse any data, they first have to extract the data from these various sources (which may include doctors' notes, hospital records, government Medicare records, etc.). Then they need to turn that information into something that computers can analyse. Clinician notes can come in many different formats – some are handwritten and some are in a scanned PDF file format – so Apixio use OCR (optical character recognition) technology to create a textual representation of that information that computers can read and understand.

Apixio work with the data using a variety of different methodologies and algorithms that are machine learning based and have natural language-processing capabilities. The data can be analysed at an individual level to create a patient data model, and it can also be aggregated across the population in order to derive larger insights around the disease prevalence, treatment patterns, etc. Schulte explains, "We create a 'patient object', essentially a profile assembled using data derived by text processing and mining text and coded healthcare data. By creating this individual profile and grouping together individuals with similar profiles, we can answer questions about what works and what doesn't in those individuals, which becomes the basis for personalized medicine."

Traditional evidence-based medicine is largely based upon studies with methodological flaws, or randomized clinical trials with relatively small populations that may not generalize well outside that particular study. By mining the world of practice-based clinical data – who has what condition, what treatments are working, etc. – organizations can learn a lot about the way they care for individuals. Schulte, a physician who was Apixio's chief medical officer before being appointed CEO, says: "I think this could positively disrupt what we [in the healthcare industry] do. We can learn more from the *practice* of medicine and refine our approach to clinical care. This gets us closer to a 'learning healthcare system'. Our thinking on what actually works and what doesn't is updated with evidence from the real-world data."

The first product to come from Apixio's technology platform is called the HCC Profiler. The customers for this product fall into two groups: insurance plans and healthcare delivery networks (including hospitals and clinics). Medicare forms a big part of their business, especially those individuals within Medicare who have opted into health maintenance organization (HMO) style plans (called Medicare Advantage Plans), which accounted for nearly 17 million individuals in the US in 2015. Health plans and physician organizations have an incentive to manage the total cost of care for these individuals. To do this, these organizations need to know much more about each individual: What are the diseases being actively treated? What is the severity of their illness? What are various treatments provided to these individuals? This is much easier to understand when you can access and mine that 80% of medical data previously unavailable for analysis, in addition to coded data found in the electronic record and in billing or administrative datasets.

## What Were The Results?

For those patients in Medicare Advantage Plans, Medicare pays a "capitated payment" to the sponsoring health plan or provider organization – a monthly payment calculated for each individual based upon the expected healthcare costs over that year. The payment is calculated using a cost prediction model that takes into account many factors, including the number, type and severity of conditions treated for the individual. Understanding these conditions is critical not just for estimating the cost of healthcare for individuals over a given period but also because the information is also very useful to help better manage care across the population. Traditionally, in order to understand such patient information, experts trained in reading charts and coding the information ("coders") would have to read the entire patient chart searching for documentation related to diseases and treatment. This is a laborious and expensive way of extracting information from patient records, and one that is fraught with human error. Apixio have demonstrated that computers can enable coders to read two or three times as many charts per hour than manual review alone. In addition to speeding up the process of chart review, Apixio have found that computers are more accurate as well. The accuracy improvement can be as high as 20% relative to what a coder manually reading the chart would be able to find themselves.

An additional benefit is the computer's ability to find gaps in patient documentation, defined as a physician notation of a chronic disease in the patient history without a recent assessment or plan. For example, over a nine-month period within a population of 25,000 patients, Apixio found over 5000 instances of diseases that were not documented clearly and appropriately. Gaps like this can lead to an inaccurate picture of disease prevalence and treatment, which can negatively affect the coordination and management of patient care. These document gaps provide a great way to better educate physicians on proper documentation. Schulte explains: "If you don't get that information right, how can the system coordinate and manage care for the individual? If you don't know what it is you're treating and who's afflicted with what, you don't know how to coordinate [care] across the population and manage it to reduce costs and improve the outcomes for individuals."

# What Data Was Used?

Apixio work with both structured and unstructured data, although the bulk of their data is unstructured, typewritten clinical charts. This can include GP notes, consultant notes, radiology notes, pathology results, discharge notes from a hospital, etc. They also work with information on diseases and procedures that are reported to the government (in this case Medicare).

# What Are The Technical Details?

Apixio's Big Data infrastructure is composed of well-known infrastructure components, which include non-relational database technology like Cassandra and distributed computing platforms like Hadoop and Spark. Apixio have added to this their own bespoke orchestration and management layer that automates a system that cannot be operated manually at the scale Apixio operate at. Everything is operated on Amazon Web Services (AWS) in the cloud, which Apixio selected for its robustness as well as its healthcare privacy and security and regulatory compliance. Everything is processed and analysed in-house using their own algorithms and machine-learning processes, as opposed to working with an external Big Data provider. Apixio created their own "knowledge graph" to recognize millions of healthcare concepts and terms and understand the relationships between them. That type of tool is healthcare-specific: an out-of-the-box solution from a Big Data provider working across a range of industries just wouldn't work for them. Patient charts in PDF or TIFF files are the primary data provided by health insurance plans, given their process for acquiring charts from provider offices via faxing, or printing and scanning the requested records in the medical office. Therefore, Apixio developed sophisticated technology to leverage and scale OCR to make machine-scanned medical charts readable by their algorithms. Sophisticated computational workflows that pre-process images, set parameters in the OCR engine and correct output had to be developed to extract the text available in a scanned chart.

## Any Challenges That Had To Be Overcome?

Getting healthcare providers and health insurance plans to share data is a real challenge, which holds back attempts to assemble large datasets for Big Data-driven knowledge generation. Apixio overcame these hurdles by demonstrating that they were offering real value. "Our value proposition is strong enough to overcome any trepidation about sharing this data … unless you solve a real critical problem today, none of these organizations will give you access to any real amount of data," Schulte explains.

Which brings us to the next challenge: data security. Thanks to some high-profile health data breaches, security is a hot topic in this field. For Apixio, the importance of data security and their legal requirements were a top consideration from the get-go. Schulte refers to data security as "table stakes", meaning it is an essential requirement for anyone wanting to operate in the healthcare Big Data arena. "For every new contract we have to demonstrate our security. And being on AWS certainly does help in that regard … it takes a good amount of their anxiety away," he explains. Patient data must be encrypted at rest and in transit, and Apixio never expose personal health information (PHI) unless access is absolutely needed by Apixio staff. "The proof is in the pudding," Schulte says. "Large health insurance plans would not sign contracts and do business with us if they didn't feel it was secure enough to do so."

## What Are The Key Learning Points And Takeaways?

Big Data in healthcare is still in its infancy, and there remains a lot of hype around the possibilities, sometimes at the expense of tangible results. Schulte confirms this: "CIOs at hospitals don't often see a lot of problems actually being solved using Big Data. They see a lot of slick dashboards which are not very helpful to them. What's helpful is actively solving problems today … for example, ensuring appropriate care and reducing costly, ineffective treatments … It's important to focus on actual results, something tangible that has been accomplished. Don't just lead with, 'Hey, I created some little whizz-bang data science tool to play with.'" This emphasis on results and outcomes is just as essential for business as it is for the healthcare industry.

If you strip away the hype, though, it's still clear that we're on the verge of exciting changes in the way we understand, treat and prevent diseases. Schulte agrees: "We're in a new world in terms of the way healthcare is going to be practised, based upon these data-driven insights, and Big Data is a way of helping us get there."

**REFERENCES AND FURTHER READING**
Find out more about Apixio and Big Data at:

http://www.apixio.com

http://www.smartdatacollective.com/bernardmarr/339832/why-we-need-more-big-data-doctors

# 7
# LOTUS F1 TEAM

*How Big Data Is Essential To The Success
Of Motorsport Teams*

## Background

Velocity is one of the defining characteristics of Big Data, and there are few situations in which speed is more imperative than motorsports. Across all levels of the sport, from NASCAR and Formula One to grassroots karting, teams and race organizers are employing ever more sophisticated data-driven strategies. In this case, we look at Formula One team Lotus F1.

## What Problem Is Big Data Helping To Solve?

Data isn't a new thing in Formula One racing: telemetry has been in use since the 1980s to stream live data from the car to engineers in the pit lane. Thomas Mayer, COO of the Lotus F1 team, tells me: "Formula One has always been on the cutting edge of technological development so it was natural that data analysis would become a big thing for us. It saves us time and money: instead of having to rely on trial and error, we have real data ..."

As well as saving the team time and money, Big Data helps them shave precious split-seconds off lap times, providing a more thrilling spectacle for spectators.

## How Is Big Data Used In Practice?

As Mayer says, "We are collecting and analysing a lot of data. We're not talking gigabytes or terabytes but petabytes."

All this data can be used to make real-time adjustments to every aspect of the car and to align it with the driver's performance. During testing, using data streamed by the cars, the team can make decisions on what to tweak or change in the car's setup before it goes back out on the track a few minutes later.

The data is also used to run simulations, which are essential as the amount of time drivers can spend practising and testing their cars is limited by the sport's governing body, the FIA, in order to create a level playing field for teams with fewer resources. The team is allowed three weeks of testing at the beginning of the year then just four days' testing throughout the season on non-racing weekends. Simulations and data analysis allow the team to turn up at a race circuit with a strong idea of how the car will perform, without having tested it – rather like looking into a crystal ball and knowing where the car will finish at the end of the race.

Just like the speed of the cars, the speed at which data is transferred is of vital importance. In 2013, Lotus F1 changed the storage provider they used for the data received by their cars to a faster system which enabled them to transfer 2000 statistics per lap. They credited this as a key factor in the dramatic improvement in performance of their junior driver Marlon Stöckinger in the Formula Renault 3.5 series; in 2013, he scored 23 points and finished 18th overall in the season; in 2014, he scored 73 points and finished ninth.

While in the early days, information would be broadcast in "packets" as the car passed the pit lane, today there is constant real-time communication. And thanks to dedicated high-speed fibre-optic lines which are laid before every race, engineers and analysts at the team's headquarters and engineering centres can have the data just a fraction of a second later than pit crews. This is important as many employees aren't actually at the circuit; for Lotus F1, which employs around 470 people, only around 60 can go to the race and only 40 of those are allowed in the race garage. This also helps the team make longer-term decisions related to the car's design and performance, rather than race-weekend tweaks.

Formula One fans generate a lot of data, too. During the 2014 US Grand Prix, spectators sent more than 2.3 terabytes of data across the mobile networks as they uploaded photos to social media and tweeted about their experience.

## What Were The Results?

While a driver has to rely on instinctive reflexes to cope with racing at 200 mph, his support team are armed with data that will prove invaluable in times of crisis. One nail-biting example of analytics coming to the rescue is when Red Bull driver Sebastian Vettel's car was spun and damaged during the 2012 Brazilian Grand Prix. By the time his car made its 10th-lap pit stop, engineers had run simulations using modelled data to determine the adjustments that would need to be made to the car to keep it running for another 70 laps. This meant Vettel won enough points to secure the championship title for a third year running.

For Lotus F1, Big Data is a key part of their success, allowing them to refine driver and car performance and increase competitiveness. It's not just about getting a good performance in one race; it's about gathering good *data* too, which helps them improve for the next race and beyond.

## What Data Was Used?

Lotus F1 naturally focus on internal data generated by their cars. Around 200 sensors attached to the car record everything from the amount of fuel that is being burned to the tyre pressure, g-force and every action by the driver (who has more than 20 controls at his fingertips). When the cars are running, they're constantly streaming data, even when in the garage, and each car logs around 50 giga-bytes of data per race. Data from the sensors is fed into mathemat-ical models, which are then analysed for insights on performance and reliability.

## What Are The Technical Details?

Lotus F1 partner with Big Data provider EMC, using their V-Block server architecture and a private cloud environment. One V-Block is located at the factory and another travels to each race. In addition, the team use a number of software tools, some of which are unique to Lotus and some of which are standard Formula One technology. For example, the car has a standard engine control unit, which comes with a set of software packages that all teams use. This is integrated with their own custom tools.

## Any Challenges That Had To Be Overcome?

The highly charged race atmosphere and trackside limitations present unique challenges for Lotus F1's IT team. Of the 40 employees allowed in the race garage, only one is an IT person. This means the systems need to be bulletproof and up and running quickly. Having one main provider simplifies things as, should anything go wrong, they only have to contact one company.

## What Are The Key Learning Points And Takeaways?

Formula One is continuously evolving, and Big Data will inevitably continue to play a part in the race for faster lap times, and greater fan engagement. As in many other areas of life, Big Data is removing a lot of the guesswork and enabling decisions to be made with the confidence that they are backed by statistics. With new technological developments such as hybrid and electric engines coming into play, things are likely to get lively in the next few years. Big Data solutions will no doubt help teams like Lotus F1 get to grips with the changes and ensure that fans are getting what they want: thrilling racing and a fast and furious spectacle.

## REFERENCES AND FURTHER READING

Find out more about the Lotus F1 team and their Big Data systems at:

http://www.v3.co.uk/v3-uk/interview/2413871/cio-insight-lotus-f1-on-superfast-big-data-and-hyper-converged-infrastructure

http://www.emc.com/microsites/infographics/emc-lotus-f1-team-infographic.htm

# 8
# PENDLETON & SON BUTCHERS[1]

## Big Data For Small Business

## Background

Pendleton & Son are a local butcher based in north-west London. Established in 1996, they have enjoyed a steady customer base and good reputation for years. Almost two years ago, when the local library closed down, a supermarket chain store moved in. Located on the same street, the new store affected overall footfall and revenue for the small butcher shop.

## What Problem Is Big Data Helping To Solve?

While founder Tom Pendleton was certain his shop offered superior quality and choice compared to the supermarket, the trouble was conveying this message to the public and getting customers through the door. Trying to compete on price wasn't working and, with falling income, son Aaron Pendleton turned to data to help keep the business afloat.

---

[1] Please note that I have changed the name of the business and people in it in order to protect their anonymity.

# How Is Big Data Used In Practice?

The Pendletons worked with a Big Data consultant who suggested installing simple, inexpensive sensors inside the store window to monitor footfall and measure the impact of window displays and promotions. Using these sensors, the firm were able to measure how many people walked past the shop, how many stopped to look at the window display and sandwich board sign and how many people then came into the store as a result. Armed with this information, they were able to refine their displays and messaging based on what interested customers the most.

The sensor data also pointed to an unexpected new revenue stream for the business. As two popular pubs were located at the end of the street, the hours of 9 p.m. to midnight proved particularly busy in terms of passers-by – almost as many as the busy lunchtime period. So the Pendletons decided to trial opening at night and serving premium hot dogs and burgers to hungry folk making their way home from the pub.

In order to decide on what products to offer at night, Aaron analysed trend data from Google Trends to see what food items were particularly popular. This led to the creation of their pulled pork burger with chorizo.

Going forward, the butchers are hoping to expand their use of data in order to increase their knowledge of customers even further. They have just started to pull in weather data to predict demand even more accurately and have plans to introduce a customer loyalty app which gathers information on who their customers are and what they purchase. This data will allow the butchers to email customers with targeted and seasonal offers. Once they have built up some customer data, surveys will allow them to delve even deeper and gain insights that can improve their products and service.

# What Were The Results?

In this case, the sensor data showed that meal suggestions on the sandwich board outside the shop, backed up by simple recipe sheets available inside, proved more popular than messages centred around price; for example, on a blustery autumn day the sign outside would read: "How about venison sausage & bean stew? Pop in for our special sausages and recipe." In short, the Pendletons found that local customers favoured inspiration and ideas over cheap deals, which were available every day in the supermarket. They were able to use this insight to improve their messaging and get more people through the door – and those who entered the shop were far more likely to make a purchase as a result.

In addition, the late-night openings proved enormously popular and the company decided to make this a permanent feature on Friday and Saturday nights. Not only did this provide much-needed additional revenue, it also introduced the company and their products to more customers.

# What Data Was Used?

The Pendletons worked with data from a small sensor placed outside the store window, plus other internal data such as transaction and stock data. They also made use of freely available external weather data to help them plan the meal suggestions and recipes for the week ahead.

# What Are The Technical Details?

For the cellular phone detection, Pendleton & Sons installed cellular phone detection sensors which detect the presence of phones through the Bluetooth and Wi-Fi signals that phones emit. The sensors work for iPhone and Android devices and pick up the MAC address of the phone, the strength of the signal (which helps you to understand the distance from the sensor), the vendor of the smartphone (e.g. Apple, Samsung) and the type of device. For the analysis, Aaron used the cloud-based business intelligence platform that the sensor vendor provided.

## Any Challenges That Had To Be Overcome?

For Aaron, the first challenge to overcome was convincing his father it was worth investing in data in the first place. It was important to make a firm business case that set out how data could help a small business like theirs. Relating data to the business's challenges and goals helped enormously with this. Aaron set out what the business wanted to achieve (i.e. increasing customer awareness and revenue), what was stopping them (competition from the supermarket and lack of information on what customers wanted) and how data could help them overcome the current challenges (by gathering the information they needed to attract more customers). Armed with a strong business plan, it was easier to argue the case for introducing data to their decision-making process.

The next challenge, which is a common one for small businesses, was knowing where to start. With limited resources and manpower, the Pendletons were always going to need someone to handle the data side of things for them. They turned to a Big-Data-as-a-service (BDAAS) provider who had experience of working with smaller businesses and, as they only paid for the work needed (as opposed to investing in new systems and staff with data experience), the initial outlay was minimal. They found the sensors themselves were surprisingly cheap (and they're getting cheaper all the time), and there was no need to invest in additional software as the BDaaS provider did all the analysis work for them.

# What Are The Key Learning Points And Takeaways?

This case study shows how Big Data isn't the sole domain of big corporations but is making a difference to businesses of all shapes and sizes. And while this type of data project isn't necessarily always seen as *Big* Data, it certainly is enabled by our Big Data world. Sometimes it simply means accessing and using the Big Data that is out there to inform your decision making. In the end, it doesn't matter how much data you gather and analyse: it's what you do with it that counts.

## REFERENCES AND FURTHER READING

You can find more information for small businesses in:

*Big Data for Small Business For Dummies* (2016), published by John Wiley & Sons, Ltd, Chichester.

And there's more on Big Data as a Service in my Forbes column:

http://www.forbes.com/sites/bernardmarr/2015/04/27/big-data-as-a-service-is-next-big-thing/

# 9
# US OLYMPIC WOMEN'S CYCLING TEAM

*How Big Data Analytics Is Used To Optimize Athletes' Performance*

## Background

As we'll see at various points in this book, sports and data analytics are becoming fast friends. In this chapter, we look at how the US women's cycling team went from underdogs to silver medallists at the 2012 London Olympics – thanks, in part, to the power of data analytics.

The team were struggling when they turned to their friends, family and community for help. A diverse group of volunteers were formed, made up of individuals in the sports and digital health communities, led by Sky Christopherson. Christopherson was an Olympic cyclist and the world record holder for the 200m velodrome sprint in the 35+ age category. He had achieved this using a training regime he designed himself, based on data analytics and originally inspired by the work of cardiologist Dr Eric Topol.

## What Problem Is Big Data Helping To Solve?

Christopherson formed his OAthlete project (as in, Optimized Athlete) after becoming disillusioned with doping in the sport. This was in the wake of the Lance Armstrong drug scandal, dubbed "the greatest fraud in American sports". The idea behind OAthlete was to help athletes optimize their performance and health in a sustainable way, without the use of performance-enhancing drugs. As a result, the philosophy "data not drugs" was born.

## How Is Big Data Used In Practice?

Working with the women's cycling team, Christopherson put together a set of sophisticated data-capture and monitoring techniques to record every aspect affecting the athletes' performance, including diet, sleep patterns, environment and training intensity. These were monitored to spot patterns related to the athletes' performance, so that changes could be made to their training programmes.

## What Were The Results?

As Christopherson says, by measuring the various aspects (such as sleep and diet) and understanding how they're related, you can create "breakthroughs in performance".

In this case, the depth of the analytics meant that Christopherson was able to drill right down to what he calls "individual optimal zones". With this information, tailored programmes could be tweaked for each athlete to get the best out of every team member. For example, one insight which came up was that the cyclist Jenny Reed performed much better in training if she had slept at a lower temperature the night before. So she was provided with a water-cooled mattress to keep her body at an exact temperature throughout the night. "This had the effect of giving her better deep sleep, which is when the body releases human growth hormone and testosterone naturally," says Christopherson. In the case of Sarah Hammer, the data revealed a vitamin D deficiency, so they made changes to her diet and daily routine (including getting more sunshine). This resulted in a measurable difference in her performance.

There's another benefit: helping athletes avoid injury. In Christopherson's opinion, the leading temptation for athletes to use the performance-enhancing drugs that have blighted cycling is the need to train hard while avoiding the dangers of injury and illness. Big Data enables high-performance sports teams to quantify the many factors that influence performance, such as training load, recovery and how the human body regenerates. This means teams can finally measure all these elements and establish early-warning signals that, for example, stop them from pushing athletes into overtraining, which often results in injury and illness. According to Christopherson, the key is finding balance during training: "It's manipulating the training based on the data you have recorded so that you are never pushing into that danger zone, but also never backing off and under-utilizing your talent. It's a very fine line and that's what Big Data is enabling us to finally do." When used accurately and efficiently, it is thought Big Data could vastly extend the careers of professional athletes and sportsmen and -women well beyond the typical retirement age of 30, with the right balance of diet and exercise and avoiding injury through overexertion.

Christopherson's system has not been put through rigorous scientific testing but it's worked well in terms of his personal success and the US women's cycling team – as demonstrated by that incredible silver medal win.

## What Data Was Used?

Christopherson worked with internal and external and structured and unstructured data; for example, time series data – like measurements of physical parameters of blood sugar, skin parameters and pulse – was captured using sensors attached to the body. These also captured noise and sunlight exposure data. Environmental data – such as temperature, time of day and weather – was also considered, using publicly available information. Video analysis was also carried out, and athletes' sleeping patterns were measured using direct EEG.

## What Are The Technical Details?

To implement the programme, Christopherson partnered with San Francisco-based data analytics and visualization specialist Datameer. The data was stored in the cloud in a Hadoop environment (HDFS), with Datameer analysing the data. Datameer's infographic widgets visualized the results.

## Any Challenges That Had To Be Overcome?

The challenge with data exploration is that it often lacks specific hypotheses. But, as Olympic athletes, the team were able to draw upon their experience and constant self-experimentation to guide the data exploration. This experience, combined with Datameer's spreadsheet approach, helped the team cope with the vast amount of data involved. Datameer's spreadsheet approach easily integrated the different types, sizes and sources of data, making it much easier to extract insights.

## What Are The Key Learning Points And Takeaways?

For me, this case study highlights the importance of finding a partner that understands the unique challenges related to your field. In this case, Datameer's CEO, Stefan Groschupf, was a former competitive swimmer at a national level in Germany. With this background and prior knowledge, Groschupf immediately saw the potential of the project. Christopherson was delighted with their input: "They came back with some really exciting results – some connections that we hadn't seen before. How diet, training and environment all influence each other. Everything is interconnected and you can really see that in the data."

It also highlights the importance of spotting patterns in the data. So, it's not just about the amount of data you collect or how you analyse it; it's about looking for patterns across different datasets and combining that knowledge to improve performance – this applies to sports teams and businesses alike.

## REFERENCES AND FURTHER READING

Find out more about OAthlete's work at:

http://www.oathlete.com/#intro and https://vimeo.com/48833290

And the amazing story of the US women's cycling team's transformation is covered in the documentary *Personal Gold*. There's more information at:

http://www.personal-gold.com/

# 10
# ZSL

*Big Data In The Zoo And To Protect Animals*

## Background

As well as running the world-famous London Zoo, ZSL are responsible for far-reaching conservation efforts around the world, in an effort to tackle the ongoing extinction threats that many species are facing.

Traditionally, most conservation work has been fieldwork carried out on the ground by zoologists and other scientists, manually tracking the movement of animal populations or the spread of vegetation using tracking devices or their own eyes.

However, with the increasing sophistication of data collection and analytics technology, along with the increasingly urgent need to take action to save an ever-growing number of species from extinction, new methods are being constantly developed to aid in the monitoring and tracking of wildlife.

Last year, ZSL together with other research organizations, including NASA and the European Commission's Joint Research Council, held the first international symposium on "remote sensing" for conservation. In essence, remote sensing involves combining the latest high-resolution satellite imagery with zoological, demographic and geographical data and advanced computer modelling and predictive analytics, to better understand the effects that human activity is having on animal and plant populations.

## What Problem Is Big Data Helping To Solve?

The threat to biodiversity from human activity is one of the biggest challenges facing us as a species. The ecosystem which we all depend on for survival is reliant on a complex balance of organisms that has developed over millions of years and makes the planet suitable for sustaining life.

The rise of humans as the dominant species on earth has had disastrous effects on the extinction rates of other species. As it is thought that as little as 15% of the plant, mammals, reptiles, fish and insect species on earth have been identified, the vast majority of these extinctions go unnoticed – it is estimated that the planet is losing as many as 140,000 species a year.

There is no way of knowing for sure what the long-term impact of this decrease in biodiversity will be. Plant and animal ecosystems interact with each other and with human life in an incredibly complex range of ways, from the food chain to the nitrogen cycle that keeps the air breathable. Creating imbalance in these processes could have potentially disastrous consequences for us as a species as well as all life on the planet.

Conservation efforts like those established by ZSL through their Institute of Zoology are essential to understanding the consequences of the damage that has already been done, and to working to mitigate it.

## How Is Big Data Used In Practice?

In recent years, thanks to huge advances in technology, computer processing power and analytical science, focus has moved to developing methods of tracking, quantifying and understanding animal populations through remote sensing.

Conservation work is hugely expensive, and vastly underfunded considering the scale of the problem. To find ways to overcome this, last year ZSL brought together experts from a wide range of scientific establishments, NGOs and charities. Graeme Buchanan of the Royal Society for the Protection of Birds (RSPB) told the symposium: "It is established that the funding available to conservation falls well short of the amount needed to address the current extinction crisis.

"Consequently, conservationists need to target funding to where it is most needed. To set priorities, the conservation community needs information on what is where and how is or might be changing. While in situ field data is invaluable, remote sensing can provide a valuable tool for delivering this information."

Plans discussed as part of the programme include using satellite imagery to track populations from space in order to track animal movement and the impact of human activity such as deforestation and urbanization.

This data can then be used with predictive modelling algorithms to anticipate future movements as well as to highlight geographical areas where animal populations are particularly at risk, or where urgent human intervention could prevent the loss of invaluable biodiversity from the planet through extinction.

Understanding animal population movement and dynamics is thought to be key to predicting the effect that human activity will have on the species we share the planet with, and data analytics is proving to be an effective tool for developing that understanding.

## What Were The Results?

Through the application of these ideas, many new frameworks have been developed that can be used by scientists around the globe to study and predict the movement of animals, and the effect manmade changes to their environment are likely to have.

Thanks to this, conservation groups, charities and political lobbyists can focus efforts on making change where it will be most effective in halting the ongoing extinction of life on earth.

## What Data Was Used?

Very high resolution (VHR) satellite imaging technology has reached the stage where images are detailed enough to show individual animals (and people). This data can then be fed into counting algorithms that quantify the size of a particular population in a particular area.

As well as quantities, migration patterns can be captured and assessed. This allows for modelling of likely migration pathways in other locations, based on data extrapolated from the observed populations.

As well as this, more down-to-earth data is also collected from camera traps, observers in the field and, increasingly, drone aircraft fitted with camera equipment.

One programme involves monitoring photographs posted by tourists and the wider public to social media, which can be scanned with image-recognition software. This software can be programmed to recognize animal or plant life, determine the location through the photo's metadata and use it to build another reference database of biodiversity within a given area.

Biological information, existing data on species distribution and human demographic data are all also used to predict and assess animal populations and how they are being affected by outside influences.

Satellite data from systems used by NASA to monitor forest fires can also be incorporated into these programmes, to monitor the effects of deforestation by fire. LiDAR technology, which replaces radar's radio waves with light waves, is used to determine the height and biomass density of vegetation in a particular area, allowing for more accurate predictions of the variety and volume of animal species inhabiting it.

## What Are The Technical Details?

Datasets collected by ZSL's migration-tracking programmes and used to inform international population indexes is hosted on Amazon Web Services (AWS) and Microsoft Azure frameworks. The society's analysts also heavily use the open-source H20 analytics platform, which allows complex analytics to be run on the distributed datasets and results to be fed back over a Web browser interface.

Dr Robin Freeman, head of indicators and assessments at the society, tells me: "Almost everyone I work with uses R [the statistical program] to some extent.

"The things you need to learn as a graduate or research student at a zoo are shifting more towards understanding statistical methods, and machine-learning programming, because it is becoming increasingly certain that you will come up against Big Data in your research."

## Any Challenges That Had To Be Overcome?

In conservation work, the biggest challenge is prioritization. With so many species disappearing at such a fast rate, it is essential that methods be developed for identifying those most at risk. This enables the efficient and effective deployment of resources, as well as the opportunity to instigate or campaign for societal changes, such as regulation, necessary to prevent loss of biodiversity.

Using data gathered through remote-sensing methods, the Wildlife Conservation Society have established a group of researchers from scientific establishments, governments and NGOs committed to identifying the 10-most-pressing problems currently facing conservationists. These include predicting future deforestation, identifying hotspots where habitat change is leading to high levels of extinction and the expense of accessing accurate data.

These priorities are used to inform global conservation efforts such as those undertaken by ZSL in order to help ensure the most effective steps are being taken.

## What Are The Key Learning Points And Takeaways?

Conservation work is vital to the future of life on earth, and Big Data analytics are an essential ingredient. Access to more accurate and timely data is improving our ability to understand and anticipate the effects human activity has on the global wildlife population, and how those changes will inevitably come back to bite us.

Data gathered through remote sensing cuts down on the need for expensive, time-consuming and sometimes dangerous fieldwork zoologists need to carry out. While ground-based sensors and manmade observations will still provide reliable data, increasingly it can be inferred from satellite imagery combined with geographic, biological and demographic data to produce accurate models and predictions.

As analytics technology becomes more advanced, we will be able to gain an increasingly clear picture of where our priorities should lie if we want to mitigate the damage we have already caused to the ecosystem.

### REFERENCES AND FURTHER READING
For more information about ZSL and Big Data, visit:

http://onlinelibrary.wiley.com/journal/10.1002/(ISSN)2056-3485; jsessionid=58CD69F2772DC42AAE9F481B7D60F3B3.f04t02

http://admin.zsl.org/sites/default/files/media/2014-06/0930%20ZSL% 20RSforConservation%20Turner%2022May2014.pdf

# 11
# FACEBOOK

## How Facebook Use Big Data To Understand Customers

## Background

Facebook, by some considerable margin, is still the world's biggest social network. It's used by everyone and their granny to keep in touch with friends, share special occasions and organize social events. Millions of people every day also use it to read news, interact with brands and make buying decisions.

Like all of the big social networks and search engines, it's essentially free to the end user. The company make the money they use to pay their 10,000-plus staff and keep their services online from businesses that pay to access the data Facebook collect on us as we use their services.

This year, the company announced they had attracted two million active advertisers, mostly small and medium-sized businesses, which pay for ads to appear in the feeds of people who may be interested in them.

## What Problem Is Big Data Helping To Solve?

Businesses need to sell products and services to survive. In order to do this, they need to find customers to sell to. Traditionally, this has been done by advertising in a "broadcast" manner: newspaper, TV, radio and display advertising work on the principle that if you put your ad in the most prominent place you can afford a large number of people will see it and some of them are likely to be interested in what you're offering.

However, this is obviously a hit-and-miss approach. For a large multinational company, it may be clear that a TV spot during the Super Bowl will increase their exposure and put their brand in front of potential customers. But a small business just starting out has to think far more carefully about the most efficient way of spending its limited marketing budget. These companies can't afford to cover all the bases, so tools that can help them work out who their customers are, and where to find them, can be hugely beneficial.

## How Is Big Data Used In Practice?

The rapid expansion of the online world over the last two decades has provided advertisers with a simple way to do just that. Because websites are hosted on computers, not newspapers or billboards, each visitor can be independently identified by the software running the website. And Facebook, with 1.5 billion active monthly users, has access to far more user data than just about anyone else.[1]

Its data is also more personal – whereas services like Google can track our Web page visits (which incidentally Facebook can now also do) and infer much about us from our browsing habits, Facebook often have full access to straight-up demographic data about us such as where we live, work, play, how many friends we have, what we do in our spare time and the particular movies, books and musicians we like.

A book publisher, for example, can then pay Facebook to put their adverts in front of a million people who like similar books, and match the demographic profiles of their customers.

Data collected by users as they browse Facebook is used to match them with companies which offer products and services that, statistically, they are likely to be interested in. Facebook undoubtedly hold one of the biggest and most comprehensive databases of personal information ever collated, and it is expanding every second of every day.

As well as a platform for sharing messages, Facebook is also a platform for running software. Over half a million apps have been created for Facebook so far, most of which take the advantage of access they have, via the extensive APIs (application program interfaces), to Facebook user data. These apps in turn gather data about how they are used that their developers use to target ads at their own customers.

Facebook also expands by buying out other companies and services and adding their data to its own. In recent years, the company have acquired the Instagram and WhatsApp services, putting more data about how we share pictures and instant messages at their disposal. More intriguingly, they also acquired virtual reality headset manufacturers Oculus. Some commentators have said this shows Facebook are interested in developing services to let us interact with each other in virtual reality, rather than simply on flat screens. Monitoring our behaviour in these new, immersive virtual worlds will undoubtedly be a very valuable source of new data in the near future.

## What Were The Results?

Facebook's tactic of leveraging their huge wealth of consumer data to sell advertising space led to their taking a 24% share of the US online display ads market in 2014, and generating $5.3 billion in revenue from ad sales. By 2017 this has been forecasted to be a 27% share, worth over $10 billion.[2]

## What Data Was Used?

Facebook, together with its users, generates its own data. Users upload 2.5 million pieces of content every minute. This content is analysed for clues about us that can be used to segment us for advertisers. Additionally, they interact with other people's content as well as data stored in Facebook's own databases, which include business listings and databases of films, music, books and TV shows. Whenever we "Like" and share this content, it learns a little bit more about us.

In order to provide privacy, all of this data is anonymized when it is fed into the systems that match businesses with potential customers. All this really means is that your name is removed and replaced with a unique identifying code which can't be traced back to you.

## What Are The Technical Details?

Facebook is the most visited Web page in the world after Google's search engine – and the most frequent thing Google is used to search for is Facebook. It is said to account for around 10% of all online traffic. Of course, a Web service of this size requires a huge amount of infrastructure.

Its data centres are filled with its custom-designed servers, built using Intel and AMD chips, and power-saving technology to help cut down the huge cost of keeping so many machines running 24/7. The designs for the server systems have been made available as open-source documentation. Facebook also relies on open-source technology for its software, which is written in PHP and runs MySQL databases. Its programmers created the HipHop for MySQL compiler, which translates PHP code into C++ at runtime, allowing code to be executed far more quickly and reducing CPU load. It uses its own distributed storage system based on Hadoop's HBase platform to manage storage. It is also known that Facebook makes use of Apache Hive for real-time analytics of user data.

## Any Challenges That Had To Be Overcome?

In line with most of the big online service providers, Facebook's biggest challenge has been gaining our trust. At the start, it wasn't unusual to find people who were highly sceptical of entering personal details into any online system, as it was impossible to know with any certainty what would be done with them. Even if every company in the world rigidly abided by the terms of their privacy and data-sharing policies, the most watertight policies in the world are powerless in the face of data loss or theft, such as hacking attacks.

From the start, Facebook attempted to win our trust by showing us they took privacy seriously. As full of holes and references to mysterious and unspecified "third parties" as they may have been, their privacy features were light years ahead of those offered by contemporaries, such as Myspace.

The fact there was at least an illusion of privacy was enough to get a lot of people on board the social media revolution. By default, anything a user shared was shared only with a trusted group of friends, in contrast to Myspace where initially posts were, by default, shared with the world. It also offered switches allowing individual aspects of a person's data to be made public or private. However, there have always been complaints that these options are confusing or difficult to find.

## What Are The Key Learning Points And Takeaways?

Facebook has revolutionized the way we communicate with each other online by allowing us to build our own network and choose who we share information about our lives with.

This data holds tremendous value to advertisers, who can use it to precisely target their products and services at people who are, according to statistics, likely to want or need them.

Targeted advertising is particularly useful to small businesses, who can't afford to waste their limited marketing budget paying for exposure to the wrong audience segment.

Gaining the trust of users is essential. Aside from data thefts and such illegal activity, users can become annoyed simply by being subjected to adverts they aren't interested in, too frequently. So it's in Facebook's interests, as well as the advertisers, to match them up effectively.

## REFERENCES AND FURTHER READING

1. Statista (2016) Number of monthly active Facebook users worldwide as of 3rd quarter 2015 (in millions), http://www.statista.com/statistics/264810/number-of-monthly-active-facebook-users-worldwide/, accessed 5 January 2016.

2. eMarketer (2015) Facebook and Twitter will take 33% share of US digital display market by 2017, http://www.emarketer.com/Article/Facebook-Twitter-Will-Take-33-Share-of-US-Digital-Display-Market-by-2017/1012274, accessed 5 January 2016.

For more information about Facebook and Big Data, visit:

http://www.wired.com/insights/2014/03/facebook-decade-big-data/

# 12
# JOHN DEERE

*How Big Data Can Be Applied On Farms*

## Background

Agricultural manufacturer John Deere have always been a pioneering company. Their eponymous founder personally designed, built and sold some of the first commercial steel ploughs. These made the lives of settlers moving into the Midwest during the middle of the 19th century much easier and established the company as an American legend. Often at the forefront of innovation, it is no surprise that they have embraced Big Data enthusiastically – assisting pioneers with the taming of the virtual wild frontier just as it did with the real one.

## What Problem Is Big Data Helping To Solve?

The world's population is growing rapidly, which means there is always going to be an increasing demand for more food. With the idea of genetically modified food still not appealing to public appetites, increasing the efficiency of the production of standard crops is key to meeting this growing demand. To this end, John Deere have launched several Big Data-enabled services that let farmers benefit from crowdsourced, real-time monitoring of data collected from their thousands of users. This data enables farmers to make informed decisions on anything from which crops to plant where to how much fertilizer to use.

# How Is Big Data Used In Practice?

Myjohndeere.com is an online portal that allows farmers to access data gathered from sensors attached to their own machinery as they work the fields, as well as aggregated data from other users around the world. It is also connected to external datasets, including weather and financial data.

These services allow farmers to make better-informed decisions about how to use their equipment, where they will get the best results from and what return on their investment they are providing.

For example, fuel usage of different combines can be monitored and correlated with their productivity levels. By analysing the data from thousands of farms, working with many different crops in many different conditions, it is possible to fine-tune operations for optimum levels of production. The system also helps to minimize downtime by predicting, based on crowdsourced data, when and where equipment is likely to fail. This data can be shared with engineers who will stand ready to supply new parts and service machinery as and when it is needed – cutting down on waste caused by expensive machinery sitting idle.

Another service is Farmsight, which the company launched in 2011. It allows farmers to make proactive decisions about what crops to plant where, based on information gathered in their own fields and those of other users. This is where certain "prescriptions" can be assigned to individual fields, or sections of fields, and machinery remotely reprogrammed to alter its behaviour according to the "best practice" suggested by the analytics.

Going forward, the company's vision is that, one day, even large farms will be manageable by a small team of humans working alongside a fleet of robotic tools, all connected and communicating with each other.

# What Were The Results?

As well as increasing farmers' profits and hopefully creating cheaper, more abundant food for the world, there are potential environmental gains, too. Pesticides and fertilizer can cause pollution of the air and waterways, so having more information on the precise levels needed for optimum production means that no more than is necessary will be used.

The potential for huge positive change – in a world facing overpopulation and an insufficient production of food – particularly in the developing nations, is something that can benefit everyone on the planet.

# What Data Was Used?

The data used is largely structured, internal data, primarily from sensors on John Deere machines and probes in the soil, which is then aggregated and made available to users of myjohndeere.com. Some external data is also provided, including weather data and financial data.

# What Are The Technical Details?

John Deere use SAP's HANA system – an in-memory, column-oriented, relational database management system – to crunch their big data. John Deere's hundreds of millions of data points are loaded into HANA and their engineers can drill into the data using analytics and mathematical models.

# Any Challenges That Had To Be Overcome?

With all of this data being generated and shared, there is a growing debate around who actually owns it. The MyJohnDeere platform lets farmers share data with each other (or choose not to, if they wish) and also with third-party application developers, who can use the APIs to connect equipment by other manufacturers, or to offer their own data analysis services. But this has not stopped many farmers asking why they should effectively pay for their own data, and asking why John Deere and other companies providing similar services shouldn't pay them – according to American Farm Bureau Federation (AFBF) director Mary Kay Thatcher.

Talks are currently ongoing between the AFBF and companies including John Deere, Monsanto and DuPont over how these concerns should be addressed. As well as privacy issues, there are concerns that having too much information could allow traders in financial markets to manipulate prices.

There's also the issue of fewer employment opportunities in agriculture as a direct result of automation and Big Data. We are starting to delegate more and more responsibilities to robots – not because farmers are lazy (as anyone who lives in an agricultural area will know, they most definitely aren't!) but because robots can often do it better. Sure, John Deere's vision of vast areas of farmland managed by a man sitting at a computer terminal with a small team of helpers will lead to fewer employment opportunities for humans working the land, but that has been the trend for at least the last century, regardless. It is a trend that started long before the advent of Big Data.

## What Are The Key Learning Points And Takeaways?

There's a common myth around Big Data that it's something only Silicon Valley companies do. Yet this case shows how any industry can benefit from data, and even the most traditional of companies are turning to Big Data. Other companies are starting to do the same, such as trucking companies using data to plan more efficient routes, real estate companies using data to predict booms and busts in the market and motor insurance companies using their customers' smartphones to track how well they really drive. These days, like John Deere, any company can become a Big Data company.

## REFERENCES AND FURTHER READING

Read more about this issue at:

> http://www.forbes.com/sites/emc/2014/07/08/who-owns-farmers-big-data/ and https://datafloq.com/read/john-deere-revolutionizing-farming-big-data/511

MyJohnDeere can be accessed at:

> https://myjohndeere.deere.com

And you can find out more about John Deere's vision for the future of farming at:

> https://www.youtube.com/watch?v=t08nOEkrX-I

# 13

# ROYAL BANK OF SCOTLAND

*Using Big Data To Make Customer Service More Personal*

## Background

Prior to the 2008 financial crisis, Royal Bank of Scotland (RBS) were at one point the largest bank in the world. When their exposure to the subprime mortgage market threatened to collapse the business, the UK Government stepped in, at one time holding 84% of the company's shares.

Currently undergoing a process of re-privatization, the bank have chosen improving customer service as their strategy to fight for their share of the retail banking market.

Big Data analysis has a key part to play in this plan. The bank have recently announced a £100 million investment in data analytics technology, and has named one of their first initiatives "personology" – emphasizing a focus on customers rather than financial products.

## What Problem Is Big Data Helping To Solve?

During the 1970s and 1980s, says RBS head of analytics Christian Nelissen, banks became detached from their customers. The focus was on pushing products and hitting sales targets, without regard as to whether they were providing their customers with the services they needed.

"In the Seventies," says Nelissen, "banks, through the agency of their branch staff and managers, knew their customers individually. They knew who they were and how they fitted in – who their family were and what they were trying to do."

At some point in the Eighties, he says, this personal relationship was lost as retail banking transitioned from helping customers look after their finances to pushing all manner of financial and insurance services in the search for new streams of revenue.

Whereas before they would have concentrated on meeting customer expectations, focus shifted to "getting products out of the door" – in Nelissen's words. Banks would have a target of selling a particular number of balance transfers or credit cards, and that's what they would try to sell to the customers who came through the door, whether or not that's what they wanted or needed.

## How Is Big Data Used In Practice?

RBS are attempting to use analytics and machines to restore a level of personal service – which at first may seem counterintuitive. But their analytics team have developed a philosophy they call "personology" in order to better understand their customers and meet their needs.

Our banks have enormous amounts of information on us available to them. Records of how we spend our money and manage our finances can give an incredibly detailed picture of how we live our lives – when and where we take vacations, get married, feel unwell and, if we are lucky enough to have any, what sort of things we spend our excess income on.

Nelissen says: "If you look at someone like Amazon, they know relatively little about their customer compared to us, but they make very good use of the data they do have.

"We've traditionally been in the opposite position – we have a huge amount of data about our customers but we're only just starting to make use of it. There's a huge richness in what we have and we're only just starting to get to the potential of it."

A very simple and straightforward example, which makes a nice starting point, is congratulating customers personally when they contact a branch on their birthday. That's not exactly Big Data analytics but it's in line with the concept of personology.

Systems have also been developed to let customers know individually how they would benefit from deals and promotions being offered. While in the past, logging into an online account, or telephoning customer services, would have been an opportunity for the bank to offer whichever services it could most profitably offload, now customers will receive personalized recommendations showing exactly how much they would save by taking up a particular offer.

Additionally, transactional data is analysed to pinpoint occurrences of customers paying twice for financial products, for example paying for insurance or breakdown assistance that is already provided as part of a packaged bank account.

## What Were The Results?

Even though it is early days, Nelissen is able to report some initial results. For example, every single customer contacted regarding duplicate financial products they were paying for opted to cancel the third-party product rather than the RBS product.

Nelissen says: "We're very excited about the stuff we are doing. We are seeing significantly improved response rates and more engagement."

*Computer Weekly* reported that one octogenarian customer was reduced to tears (as were members of the bank staff) when he was wished a happy birthday: no one else had remembered.[1] While looking at isolated examples may seem counter to the philosophy of Big Data, it's immensely important to remember that ultimately it is the way in which strategies such as this affect people on an individual basis.

## What Data Was Used?

RBS use data on their customers, including their account transactional history and personal information, to determine what products or services would be most useful.

## What Are The Technical Details?

The bank use analytics-based CRM software developed by Pegasystems to make real-time recommendations to staff in branches and call centres about how to help specific customers. They have also built their own dashboards using SAS and use open-source technology, including Hadoop (supplied by Cloudera) and Cassandra.

## Any Challenges That Had To Be Overcome?

According to Nelissen, getting staff on board was one of the major challenges faced at the start. "We're at the point where the staff feel like they are having valuable conversations with their customers.

"They're at the point where they understand what the data is trying to do and feel it helps them have good conversations – and that's a big shift from where we were before.

"Staff engagement is critical – the ideas that work best, and that have the best resonance with customers, are the ones that we either got from the frontline or we worked really closely with the frontline to develop."

## What Are The Key Learning Points And Takeaways?

In sales and marketing terms, data is useless if it doesn't tell us something we don't already know about our customers.

By understanding customers better, organizations can position themselves to better meet their needs.

Engaging with staff and other stakeholders is essential. They must fully understand the reason that data analytics is being used in customer-facing situations if they are going to make the most effective use of the insights being uncovered.

### REFERENCES AND FURTHER READING

1. Goodwin, B. (2015) Royal Bank of Scotland goes back to 1970s values with big data, http://www.computerweekly.com/news/4500248239/Royal-Bank-of-Scotland-goes-back-to-1970s-values-with-big-data, accessed 5 January 2016.

# 14
# LINKEDIN

## *How Big Data Is Used To Fuel Social Media Success*

## Background

LinkedIn is the world's largest online professional network, with more than 410 million members in over 200 countries. LinkedIn connects professionals by enabling them to build a network of their connections and the connections of their connections. The site was launched by Reid Hoffman in 2003, making it one of the oldest social media networks in the world.

## What Problem Is Big Data Helping To Solve?

Competition among social networks is fiercer than ever and what's hot one year may not be the next. LinkedIn need to ensure their site remains an essential tool for busy professionals, helping them become more productive and successful, whether they're using the premium (paid-for) service or the free service. As such, Big Data is at the very heart of LinkedIn's operations and decision making, helping them provide the best possible service for the site's millions of members.

## How Is Big Data Used In Practice?

LinkedIn track every move users make on the site: every click, every page view, every interaction. With 410 million members, that's an awful lot of events to process each day. Data scientists and researchers at LinkedIn analyse this mountain of data in order to aid decision making, and design data-powered products and features. I could fill a whole book on the many ways LinkedIn use Big Data, but here I just want to look at a few key examples.

Much like other social media networks, LinkedIn use data to make suggestions for their users, such as "people you may know". These suggestions are based on a number of factors, for example if you click on someone's profile (in which case, it's reasonable to assume you may know them, or someone else by that name), if you worked at the same company during the same period or if you share some connections. Also, because users can upload their email contacts, LinkedIn use this information to make suggestions – not only for the people *you* may know on the site but also for people *your contacts* may know when they join the site. LinkedIn can also pull data about users from other sites, such as Twitter, to make suggestions about people you may know.

LinkedIn use machine-learning techniques to refine their algorithms and make better suggestions for users. Say, for example, LinkedIn regularly gave you suggestions for people you may know who work at Company A (which you worked at eight years ago) and Company B (which you worked at two years ago). If you almost never click on the profiles of people from Company A but regularly check out the suggestions from Company B, LinkedIn will prioritize Company B in their suggestions going forward. This personalized approach enables users to build the networks that work best for them.

One of the features that set LinkedIn apart from other social media platforms like Facebook is the way it lets you see who has viewed your profile. And this feature recently got a lot more detailed: while you used to be able to see how many had viewed your profile and who the most recent viewers were, now you can also see what regions and industries those viewers are from, what companies they work for and what keywords (if any) brought them to your profile. These insights, made possible by Big Data, help users increase their effectiveness on the site.

LinkedIn use stream-processing technology to ensure the most up-to-date information is displayed when users are on the site – from information on who's joined the site and who got a new job to useful articles that contacts have liked or shared. In a nutshell, the site is constantly gathering and displaying new data for users. Not only does this constant streaming of data make the site more interesting for users, it also speeds up the analytic process. Traditionally, a company would capture data and store it in a database or data warehouse to be analysed at a later time. But, with real-time stream-processing technology, LinkedIn have the potential to stream data direct from the source (such as user activity) and analyse it on the fly.

Finally, let's not forget that LinkedIn need to pull in the revenue, and they do this through recruitment services, paid membership and advertising. Big Data has a role to play in increasing revenue as well as improving the user experience. For example, in advertising – which accounts for 20–25% of LinkedIn's annual revenue – analysts work with LinkedIn's sales force to understand why members click on certain ads and not others. These insights are then fed back to advertisers in order to make their ads more effective.

## What Were The Results?

LinkedIn's success metrics include revenue and number of members, both of which continue to rise year on year. LinkedIn gained 40 million new members in the first half of 2015 and, at the time of writing, the company's most recent quarterly revenue stood at over $700 million (up from around $640 in the previous quarter). There's no doubt that Big Data plays a large role in the company's continued success.

## What Data Was Used?

LinkedIn track every move their users make on the site, from everything liked and shared to every job clicked on and every contact messaged. The company serve tens of thousands of Web pages every second of every day. All those requests involve fetching data from LinkedIn's backend systems, which in turn handle millions of queries per second. With permission, LinkedIn also gather data on users' email contacts.

## What Are The Technical Details?

Hadoop form the core of LinkedIn's Big Data infrastructure, and are used for both ad hoc and batch queries. The company have a big investment in Hadoop, with thousands of machines running map/reduce jobs. Other key parts of the LinkedIn Big Data jigsaw include Oracle, Pig, Hive, Kafka, Java and MySQL. Multiple data centres are incredibly important to LinkedIn, in order to ensure high availability and avoid a single point of failure. Today, LinkedIn run out of three main data centres.

LinkedIn have also developed their own open-source tools for Big Data access and analytics. Kafka started life this way, and other developments include Voldemort and Espresso (for data storage) and Pinot (for analytics). Open-source technology like this is important to LinkedIn because they feel it creates better code (and a better product) in the long run.

In addition, the company have an impressive team of in-house data scientists – around 150 at current estimates. Not only do the team work to improve LinkedIn products and solve problems for members, they also publish at major conferences and contribute to the open-source community. In fact, the team are encouraged to actively pursue research in a number of areas, including computational advertising, machine learning and infrastructure, text mining and sentiment analysis, security and SPAM.

## Any Challenges That Had To Be Overcome?

When you think that LinkedIn started with just 2700 members in their first week, massive data growth is one obvious challenge LinkedIn continually have to overcome – the company now have to be able to handle and understand enormous amounts of data every day. The solution to this is in investing in highly scalable systems, and ensuring that the data is still granular enough to provide useful insights. Hadoop provide the back-end power and scalability needed to cope with the volumes of data, and LinkedIn's user interface allows their employees to slice and dice the data in tons of different ways.

From a company that employed fewer than 1000 employees five years ago, LinkedIn have grown to employ almost 9000 people. This places enormous demand on the analytics team. Perhaps in response to this, LinkedIn recently reorganized their data science team so that the decision sciences part (which analyses data usage and key product metrics) now comes under the company's chief financial officer, while the product data science part (which develops the LinkedIn features that generate masses of data for analysis) is now part of engineering. As such, data science is now more integrated than ever at LinkedIn, with analysts becoming more closely aligned with company functions.

It may come as a surprise to learn that hiring staff is also a challenge, even for a giant like LinkedIn. Speaking to CNBC.com, LinkedIn's head of data recruiting, Sherry Shah, confirmed they were looking to hire more than 100 data scientists in 2015 (a 50% increase from 2014). But competition for the best data scientists is tough, especially in California, and Shah admitted that "there is always a bidding war". Although more people are entering the field, it's likely this skills gap – where demand for data scientists outstrips supply – will continue for a few years yet.

In addition, LinkedIn haven't escaped the privacy backlash. In June 2015, the company agreed to pay $13 million to settle a class action lawsuit resulting from sending multiple email invitations to users' contact lists. As a result of the settlement, LinkedIn will now explicitly state that their "Add Connections" tool imports address books, and the site will allow those who use the tool to select which contacts will receive automated invitations and follow-up emails.

## What Are The Key Learning Points And Takeaways?

As one of the oldest social media networks and still going strong, LinkedIn provide a lesson to all businesses in how Big Data can lead to big growth. Their ability to make suggestions and recommendations to users is particularly enviable (and is also used successfully by other companies featured in this book, such as Etsy and Airbnb). But LinkedIn also provide an example of the need for transparency when using individuals' data – and the backlash that can occur when people feel a company isn't being entirely transparent. I think we can expect to see more lawsuits like this against companies in future so it's important to be crystal clear with your customers what data you are gathering and how you intend to use it.

### REFERENCES AND FURTHER READING
There's more on LinkedIn's use of Big Data at:

https://engineering.linkedin.com/big-data

https://engineering.linkedin.com/architecture/brief-history-scaling-linkedin

http://www.cnbc.com/2015/06/04/big-data-is-creating-big-career-opportunites.html

http://venturebeat.com/2014/10/31/linkedin-data-science-team/

http://www.mediapost.com/publications/article/251911/linkedin-to-pay-13-million-to-settle-battle-over.html

# 15
# MICROSOFT
*Bringing Big Data To The Masses*

## Background

Microsoft have a strong track record for correctly predicting mainstream trends in computing. Just as they foresaw and cashed in on the rise of the personal computer, the graphical operating system and the Internet, they have been forecasting the growing importance of Big Data analytics for many years.

Critics may claim that innovation is not Microsoft's strong point, but they can't deny that packaging and selling it to the mainstream certainly is. Current CEO Satya Nadella has shown himself to be just as astute as his predecessors in this regard, steering the company in the direction of becoming a data-as-a-service infrastructure provider.

## What Problem Is Big Data Helping To Solve?

Big Data is really nothing new: data and analytics have existed for a long time and we've always combined them. What has changed, thanks to technology and ever-increasing connectedness, is the size and speed of the data, and the sophistication of the analytics.

However, one problem still looms large for anyone who hits on the idea of using data and analytics to solve problems. Data analytics, particularly Big Data analytics – which involves working with huge, constantly changing and highly complex datasets – is difficult.

Unless you are an accomplished statistician and computer programmer, it's likely, if you've conceived a valuable application of data analytics within your business, that you're going to need help putting it to work for you. Algorithms have to be written and a hardware framework needs to be built to store the data, run your analysis and report the results.

This gaping chasm between what people are capable of conceiving and what they are capable of building has led to the emergence of many businesses offering "data-as-a-service" (DAAS) or "software-as-a-service" (SAAS) solutions. Here, Microsoft are once again at the forefront, just as they were with offering operating systems like MS-DOS and then Windows, commercial productivity software such as their Office suite and Web browsers.

Additionally, Microsoft have shown that they have their sights on the increasingly competitive and lucrative online advertising market. Microsoft have seen their competitors, such as Google, Apple and Amazon, carve out their own highly profitable segments, and have been after their own for a while. Microsoft's search engine, Bing, while still some way behind, is gaining ground on market leader Google. And while many cheered the company's decision to make the latest version of Windows OS available as a free upgrade to existing users, they undoubtedly had less-than-altruistic, business-driven reasons for doing so.

Windows 10 heralds the rollout of their Advertiser ID protocol across their home OS business, meaning each user is assigned an individual, anonymous identifier to collect data that can be sold to help advertisers with their targeted marketing strategies.

# How Is Big Data Used In Practice?

Microsoft's enterprise software and DAAS packages offer everything to cloud-hosted versions of perennial favourites such as Word and Excel, to Hadoop-based analytics platforms and their own machine-learning algorithms aimed at serious Big Data projects.

Their Analytics Platform System is sold as a "Big Data in a box" solution that combines their SQL Server database system with their HDInsight Hadoop distribution. Similar to services offered by Amazon, IBM and Google, they supply cloud-based platforms, meaning there is no need for smaller companies to invest in their own data warehousing hardware, as well as cloud-based computing power to crunch through that data. They also offer consulting services to help businesses put them to proper use.

Microsoft Azure is another as-a-service framework specifically marketed towards Internet of Things (IoT) projects. Azure is built to handle "intelligent" machine-to-machine communications, enabling everyday industrial and consumer items to become smarter by communicating and even learning from each other. Executives, including Nadella, have made it clear that they believe the IoT is the future, and the latest version of Windows comes in a specially formulated version, created specifically to run on IoT devices. So expect to see Windows running on all manner of everyday devices in the near future.

Possibly eclipsing all of that, however, in terms of how it will speed up the encroachment of analytics into all areas of life, is Microsoft's Power BI toolset. With this, Microsoft are putting advanced, Big Data-driven analytics into the hands of the millions of users of their Office products by integrating advanced analytics functionality into Excel, the world's most widely used spreadsheet and data analysis software. And why not? After all, Excel introduced basic data interrogation and reporting into the skillset of admin-level office workers around the world, so introducing them to Big Data is the logical next step.

Inside the home, Microsoft, in line with their competitors, are concentrating their strategy on gathering as much data as they possibly can about their users. This is done to serve two purposes: refining their products and services based on user feedback and gathering data to sell to advertisers.

The release of Windows 10 caused widespread concern over the amount of data the OS appears to collect and send back to Microsoft. Default settings allow it to monitor data about activities online, such as Web pages visited, as well as offline, such as from files stored on your computer's hard drive. Online security experts were quick to urge users to alter these settings as soon as possible.

In terms of refining their products, Microsoft can use data gathered in this way to understand what users do with their software, and how it could be made more useful. The development of features and options that are rarely used can be scaled back to concentrate resources on those that provide users with most value. In the pre-Big Data days, software vendors often only had one way of gauging user satisfaction: whether or not they upgraded to a new version of a product. Today, feedback on how an application, or operating system, is used, is available instantaneously in real-time.

## What Were The Results?

Microsoft have quickly risen to be one of the most prominent and successful sellers of cloud-based, software and DAAS platforms and infrastructure. Last year, they generated revenues of $6.3 billion from cloud-based enterprise services, which they have forecasted to grow to $20 billion by 2018.[1]

It seems fears over privacy and being spied on by our own computers did not put us off our free upgrades to Windows 10. Three weeks after the OS was released in July 2015, it had been downloaded 53 million times.

## What Data Was Used?

Within their own products, Microsoft collect data regarding who we are, based on our Web-surfing habits and social media "likes", as well as how we use their software. Windows 10 can monitor how long we spend listening to music or watching videos through the inbuilt apps in the OS, as well as what hardware we are running them on and what other software is installed. If you use the Cortana voice-control features, it also records and stores what was said for analysis, to allow it to improve its own language ability.

It also collects "experience data" related to how you use your computer, and how it reacts. This includes the frequency of software crashes you experience, or the response time from clicking a particular button to performing the task you want it to do.

Microsoft are open in their terms and conditions about the data they collect in Windows 10.[2] However, the distinction about what data is used for internally improving the performance of software and what data is sold to advertisers is very blurry, as the policy document stands at the time of writing.

## What Are The Technical Details?

Microsoft claim that over 10 trillion objects (files) are now stored on their Azure cloud network, up from four trillion in 2012. In 2013, they announced they had reached one million servers spread across their more than 100 worldwide data centres, with the largest, in Chicago, containing a quarter of a million servers. As well as the Azure cloud infrastructure, these data centres provide storage and access to data created by Microsoft's 200 online services including Bing, Outlook, Office365 as well as the Xbox Live gaming network.

## Any Challenges That Had To Be Overcome?

A lack of their own smartphone platform put Microsoft at a disadvantage next to their major competitors: Google and Apple. The company sought to overcome this with the purchase of Nokia in 2014, but so far have failed to achieve a major presence in that market. They will be hoping this year's launch of Windows 10 as a cross-platform OS – integrating a user's experience across their desktop, tablet and phone – will rectify this given time.

## What Are The Key Learning Points And Takeaways?

Microsoft clearly understand it is vital that the many businesses of all shapes and sizes around the globe which use their products can see the value of their latest, Big Data-driven services.

While big business and industry have enthusiastically adopted analytics across the board, smaller enterprise, with fewer resources, has been more cautious. Microsoft generated enormous revenues selling their enterprise OS and productivity software to small and medium-sized businesses. They clearly saw they had to achieve the same penetration with their Big Data services to retain their position as a major tech player.

A careful balance must be struck between gathering data to improve user experience and spying. Microsoft generated a fair bit of negative coverage over the default privacy settings in Windows 10, but that didn't stop more than 50 million people installing it in just a few weeks. The point at which that balance between privacy and utility should be set has not yet been established – companies are using that to their huge advantage at the moment, but this could be a risky strategy in the long term. The potential fallout of getting it wrong could be disastrous, even for a giant like Microsoft.

## REFERENCES AND FURTHER READING

1. Noyes, N. (2015) Microsoft's Nadella sets lofty cloud goals, http://www
   .computerworlduk.com/news/cloud-computing/microsofts-nadella-sets-
   lofty-cloud-goals-3610084/, accessed 5 January 2016.
2. Microsoft (2015) Privacy statement, http://windows.microsoft.com/en-
   us/windows/preview-privacy-statement, accessed 5 January 2016.

# 16
# ACXIOM

*Fuelling Marketing With Big Data*

## Background

Acxiom are sometimes referred to as "the biggest company you've never heard of". They were responsible for revolutionizing the US direct-marketing industry during the 1980s by applying computerized advanced analytics across massive datasets – making them a genuine Big Data pioneer long before the term "Big Data" became fashionable.

The company's website says they hold data on "all but a small percentage" of US households. To research this chapter, I spoke to Charles Morgan, who was responsible for transforming a small company of analysts providing services to local businesses into a multinational Big Data-driven powerhouse with a billion-dollar turnover.

Initially named Demographics, the company were founded in 1969 as a sideline by Charles D. Ward, chairman of his family's regional school bus company. Ward's initial idea was to collect data and manage a mailing list for the local Democrat party. When the school bus company hit financial difficulties and Ward was threatened with bankruptcy, he sold his shares to Charles Morgan, his employee, and a graduate of the University of Arkansas who had formerly worked as an IBM systems engineer.

## What Problem Is Big Data Helping To Solve?

During the 1980s, the banks moved their businesses heavily into retail. They began trying to sell as many credit cards, insurance packages, bank accounts and financial services as they could think of, to as many people as possible.

Businesses had long been contacting customers directly in order to offer products they thought would appeal, and the term "direct marketing" was coined in 1967. But what the US banks, such as Citibank, which became Acxiom's biggest customer, needed was more complicated than anything that had been done before. With all the major banks more or less simultaneously deciding to pursue the same market, even with direct-marketing budgets in the hundreds of millions of dollars, there was no margin for error and every cent would have to be spent efficiently.

Morgan tells me: "There were a lot of issues with large-scale data management. We were able to observe the lists people in the data business had and it was all highly manual.

"There was no real analysis on any sophisticated level. I looked at the problem and thought, this is a great opportunity to deploy modern computer science to a problem that's going to get bigger and bigger as people figure out how to do a more efficient job of direct marketing."

In order to cope with the huge amount of data, which included information on virtually every US citizen gathered from the three major credit agencies, Acxiom vastly upgraded their analytics and data management capabilities and focused on developing more-efficient algorithms to effectively segment the population. Morgan says: "The relationship with Citibank grew and we were handling direct marketing of all of their credit card products. We did all kinds of analytics, for their current projects and ones they were working on for the future, and that's how we really got into the Big Data business: they kept wanting more and more data and more and more analytics, and we had to work out how to satisfy their needs."

## How Is Big Data Used In Practice?

Acxiom created their proprietary list order fulfilment system, which took data from the credit agencies and combined it into the first online mailing list generator. This provided businesses with millions of unique, named leads, segmented by age, location, profession, industry or any other known information.

Morgan says: "We had to build very large data warehouses. We were getting data by the month on the entire population from the credit bureaus and combining that with historical data and current data about where they had lived, how many children in the family – if they'd been a 10-year customer but had recently stopped being a customer, we knew that.

"We often knew what magazines they subscribed to. The amount of data we amassed was almost unimaginable. There would be over 100 million people in just one of these databases and we'd have to build entirely new versions three times a year. With data on so many people from so many sources, there would be a lot of conflicting data and we would have to establish what was accurate. Plus, it wasn't really legal to build a credit database: you had to build it for a specific purpose [e.g. marketing] so it was also driven by legal requirements. We didn't have the term 'Big Data' back then; we just called them 'very large databases.' "

Since pioneering Big Data-driven marketing, Acxiom have moved with the times. In 2010, they unveiled their PersonicX system, which analyses a person's public social media activity to match them to particular consumer profiles, and combining this with their other data to more precisely match them with products and services they may need. Acxiom outsource these services to businesses around the world from global financial giants to small businesses.

## What Were The Results?

Charles Morgan built up Acxiom from a 27-employee company to a business employing over 7000 people by pioneering data and analytics-driven direct marketing. Today, they are said to generate 12% of the revenue of the entire US direct-marketing industry, amounting to around $1.15 billion a year.

## What Data Was Used?

Acxiom take their data on citizens in the US and around the world from credit agencies as well as public records such as electoral rolls, marriage and birth registers, consumer surveys and from thousands of other businesses and organizations that collect data on their customers and service users, and pass it on (when those customers fail to "opt out" at the right moment!).

Although they do not collect information themselves on individuals' Web-surfing behaviour, they do buy in information from other organizations that do – so long as the relevant privacy and security regulations are in place. This means they undoubtedly have a lot of information on our online activity too.

One area of online activity which they do monitor, however, is social media, which is increasingly becoming a very fertile source of insights into consumer sentiment and behaviour.

# What Are The Technical Details?

One of the first things Acxiom did when they realized the scale of the data problem they had on their hands was to develop their own SQL-like language to let them query the datasets they were collecting, which they named Select Language.

Most of the early pioneering data work was done with tape-based systems, but when Citibank dramatically scaled up the requirements for analytics power and storage, Acxiom invested heavily in DEC Alpha supercomputers running Oracle to implement their first truly Big Data-oriented systems. Morgan says: "This was a transformational gain for us. It meant we could really start carrying out the sort of analysis we had wanted to do but had been held back by the speed of existing hardware."

At one point, the company operated server farms taking up a total of six acres of land, spread across the US and around the world. Today, their Arkansas headquarters is said to contain 23,000 servers, storing around 1500 data points on half a billion people.

# Any Challenges That Had To Be Overcome?

Morgan says that the biggest challenge during the 1980s was keeping up with the company's phenomenal growth following their partnership with Citibank in 1983, and the other major partnerships that quickly followed.

He says: "Our biggest problem for most of our history was managing our growth. When you increase in size by orders of magnitude in eight or nine years and don't have a model to follow – it's almost like, 'Oh my god, we've got another customer, we don't have enough computer capacity, what are we going to do? Through the Eighties and Nineties, most of our problems came about through managing our growth.'"

Of course, with a business model based on pioneering new ways of collecting and selling on personal data on private citizens, controversy was always bound to rear its head on occasion.

The company have been accused of sharing data without consent by the US Federal Trade Commission, questioned over the "opt out" facilities that they are legally obliged to provide and nominated for a Big Brother Award as "worst corporate invader for a tradition of data brokering".

They have responded to this by ramping up their confidentiality and data-protection policies in recent years and creating the website aboutthedata.com, which explains how, when and where they collect and use personal data.

## What Are The Key Learning Points And Takeaways?

Increasingly sophisticated methods of applying advanced analytics to demographic data are giving sellers more and more power to put their brand in front of the best potential customers, at the right time.

Technology has driven this increase in analytical power – which was in turn driven by the need of big business to more accurately target customers.

Big Data analytical techniques such as those developed by Acxiom have delivered tremendous growth to the businesses that adopted them in recent decades.

They also raise vital privacy concerns. Although much has been done by the direct-marketing industry and those that collect and interpret data on its behalf to gain public trust, a lot more will need to be done in the future in order to keep it.

## REFERENCES AND FURTHER READING

To find out more about Acxiom's founder see:

http://www.amazon.com/Matters-Life-Data-Remarkable-Visionary/dp/1630474657/

For more on the way Acxiom use customer data visit:

http://www.nytimes.com/2012/06/17/technology/acxiom-the-quiet-giant-of-consumer-database-marketing.html

# 17

# US IMMIGRATION AND CUSTOMS

## How Big Data Is Used To Keep Passengers Safe And Prevent Terrorism

## Background

People move back and forward across US borders at a rate of nearly 100 million crossings a year. The Department of Homeland Security (DHS) have the unenviable task of screening each one of those crossings to make sure they aren't being made with ill intentions, and pose no threat to national security.

Federal agencies have spent many millions of dollars since 11 September 2001, in the hope that they can prevent terrorists entering the country and carrying out further attacks on domestic soil. While formerly airport security measures focused on detecting the transportation of dangerous items such as drugs or bombs, the emphasis has shifted towards identifying bad people.

Working together with researchers at the University of Arizona, the DHS have developed a system which they call the Automated Virtual Agent for Truth Assessments in Real time – AVATAR.[1]

## What Problem Is Big Data Helping To Solve?

Since 9/11, the US has been increasingly aware that among the millions of people crossing its borders every year are some who are travelling with the intention of doing harm.

Security has been massively stepped up at airports and other points of entry, and generally this relies on one-to-one screening carried out by human agents, face-to-face with travellers.

This of course leaves the system open to human fallibility. Immigrations and Customs Service officers are highly trained to notice inconsistencies and telltale signs that a person may not be being honest about their reason for entering the country, and what they intend to do when they get there. However, of course, as with anything involving humans, mistakes will happen.

Research has shown that there is no foolproof way for a human to tell whether another human is lying simply by speaking to and watching them, despite what many believe about "give-away signs". Compounding this problem, humans inevitably get tired, bored or distracted, meaning their level of vigilance can drop.

Of course, none of this is a problem to a computer. It will examine the final traveller of the day with the same vigilance and alertness as it did when it started work in the morning.

## How Is Big Data Used In Practice?

The AVATAR system uses sensors that scan the person's face and body language, picking up the slightest variations of movement or cues which could suggest something suspicious is going on. In addition, a computerized "agent" with a virtual, human face and voice asks several questions in spoken English. The subject of the inspection answers, and their response is monitored to detect fluctuations in tone of voice, as well as the content of what exactly was said.

This data is then compared against the ever-growing and constantly updating Big Database collected by AVATAR, and matched against "suspicious" profiles which experience has shown can indicate that someone has something to hide or is not being honest about their intentions in travelling.

Should it match a "suspicious" profile, the subject is highlighted for further inspection, this time carried out by a human agent.

The data is fed back to the human agents via tablets and smartphones, which gives them a probabilistic assessment of whether a particular subject is likely to be being honest – each aspect of their profile is coded red, amber or green – depending on how likely AVATAR believes it is that they are being truthful. If too many reds or ambers flash up, that subject will be investigated in more depth.

As well as on the US–Mexico border, the AVATAR system has been trialled on European borders, including at Bucharest's main airport, Henri Coandă International, Romania.[2]

## What Were The Results?

Field tests of the AVATAR system were carried out by the National Center for Border Security and Immigration in Nogales, Arizona, which concluded that the machine was capable of carrying out the task it had been designed for. As a result, it has been cleared by security to be put into operation in several jurisdictions in the US and Europe.

## What Data Was Used?

The AVATAR system relies on three sensors built into its cabinet to make probabilistic judgements about whether a person is telling the truth. The first is an infrared camera that records data on eye movements and pupil dilation at 250 frames per second. A video camera monitors body language for suspicious twitches or habitual movements of the body that fit profiles which people tend to adopt when they are hiding something. Lastly, a microphone records voice data, to listen for subtle changes in the pitch and tone of voice.

## What Are The Technical Details?

The system combines audio and video data-capture devices with a database of human cues that can give insight into whether the interviewee is acting in a suspicious manner. It is a kiosk-based system with everything needed for operation included in one unit, making it simple to set up and move to different points of immigration around the world, where fast data networks may not be available. The infrared eye movement sensor collects images at 250 frames per second to catch tiny movements that would never be visible to another human.

## Any Challenges That Had To Be Overcome?

Working out whether human beings are lying is notoriously difficult. Despite having existed since the early 20th century in some form, no lie detector (polygraph) has ever been shown to be 100% reliable, and courts have never accepted that they are accurate enough for their findings to be presented as evidence in the US or Europe.

AVATAR aims to overcome this through a process similar to the predictive modelling techniques used in many Big Data projects. As it examines more people, it learns more about the facial, vocal and contextual indicators likely to be present when a person is being dishonest. While a traditional lie detector relies on human interpreters to match these signals to what they feel, based on their experience and the limited amount of reference data they have access to. By interviewing millions of people every year, AVATAR should build up a far more reliable set of reference data which it can use to flag up suspicious travellers.

# What Are The Key Learning Points And Takeaways?

Levels of migration both in and out of the US are constantly increasing, and systems like AVATAR can relieve the manpower burden required to carry out essential safety screening on travellers.

Machines have the capability to detect whether humans are lying or acting deceptively, far more accurately than people themselves can, if they are given the right data and algorithms.

Humans respect authority – lab tests on the AVATAR system found that interviewees were more likely to answer truthfully when AVATAR was given a serious, authoritative tone and face than when programmed to speak and appear friendly and informal.[3]

It will always be possible for a human to cheat the system by effectively adopting deceptive strategies. However, the chances of being able to do so successfully will reduce as technology like AVATAR becomes more efficient and widely deployed.

## REFERENCES AND FURTHER READING

1. University of Arizona (2016) AVATAR: Automated Virtual Agent for Truth Assessments, in Real-Time, http://borders.arizona.edu/cms/projects/avatar-automated-virtual-agent-truth-assessments-real-time, accessed 5 January 2016.
2. University of Arizona (2014) University of Arizona – UA Developed Avatar is Helping to Screen New Arrivals at Bucharest Airport, http://uanews.org/story/ua-developed-avatar-is-helping-to-screen-new-arrivals-at-bucharest-airport, accessed 5 January 2016.
3. Neyfakh, L. (2014) Can a robot be too nice?, http://www.bostonglobe.com/ideas/2014/08/15/artificial-agents/YHi20t50sS4bhj0so98OZK/story.html, accessed 5 January 2016.

# 18
# NEST

*Bringing The Internet of Things Into The Home*

## Background

The Internet of Things (IoT) is an idea that has been gathering steam for a while but has burst into full fruition over the last couple of years. In a nutshell, its name comes from the fact that the original Internet we are all now used to having in our lives was based around computers talking to each other. With computers becoming smaller, more powerful and integrated in more and more everyday objects (phones being only the most ubiquitous example), just about everything can talk to each other digitally. So instead of an Internet made up of computers, we have an Internet made up of … things!

The idea is particularly applicable to household items, which is why "smart" versions of everyday tools and gadgets are emerging on the market at an ever-increasing rate. These include smart televisions, bathroom scales, sports equipment, kitchen utensils and even lightbulbs.

Nest are a company that have made a name for themselves during this first incursion of intelligent machines into our homes. Their products – smart thermostats, smoke and carbon monoxide detectors and most recently security cameras – are installed in thousands of homes. In 2013, the company were acquired by Google, a move analysts interpreted as signalling the search-engine giant's interest in developing an "operating system for the home".[1]

## What Problem Is Big Data Helping To Solve?

A huge amount of energy is wasted through inefficient home heating systems. Much of the time, this is down to user error rather than faults. Our lives follow erratic patterns but we always want to wake up to a warm home in the winter. However, a lot of the time we programme our thermostats based on nothing more than guesswork. "Dumb" thermostats simply do what you tell them: switching on at a set time and off at a set time. This causes inefficiencies because our activity patterns change from day to day and regular schedules are often a luxury many of us do without in our hectic 21st-century lives. There are other hazards to avoid, such as water freezing in pipes during unexpected cold spells when houses are left empty, leading to damage and costly repair bills.

In addition, energy firms have a role to play in preventing energy waste. They are responsible for ensuring a sufficient supply is available during times of peak use, while minimizing energy distributed from the grid to areas where it is not needed.

## How Is Big Data Used In Practice?

The Nest thermostat "learns" the most efficient strategy for keeping your home at a comfortable temperature by monitoring your daily activity and teaching itself to suit you.

Every time you set the temperature (which is done with a simple dial), it records your action and the time of day. It also uses motion sensors to record when you are home and when you are out. Gradually, it begins to understand your activity patterns and to work out the best routine for your home heating system to follow. It can integrate with any home heating system and is able to dynamically adjust the temperature to keep it at a comfortable level, based on its understanding of what you are doing. Differences in the time it takes individual heating systems to heat a home to a required temperature are also taken into account, to further cut down on wasted energy. For example, if it knows you regularly leave the home at 9 a.m. and your heating system keeps the home warm for an hour later, it can learn to switch it off at 8 a.m.

Beyond that, the smart thermostat can also be tapped into by energy companies and controlled remotely. Many providers are offering deals such as free thermostats to home owners, on condition they give permission for the companies to take control of them at certain times, to cope with peaks and drops in demand on energy from the network. The energy companies pay Nest around $50 for each customer who signs up to these deals, as the savings they are able to generate by regulating usage at peak times more than compensates for the loss.

## What Were The Results?

According to Nest founder and CEO Tony Fadell, their arrangement with power companies to allow them to regulate supply reduces energy wastage by up to 50% in the areas where they operate.[2]

In early 2015, three studies into the savings made by customers with Nest thermostats in their homes found that the devices cut heating costs by between 10 and 12% and cooling costs, in homes with air conditioning, by around 15%.[3]

## What Data Was Used?

The Nest thermostat gathers information from the user at setup, such as location data and whether the property it is installed in is a home or a business. Sensors in the thermostat collect data on temperature and humidity, as well as light levels, which it uses to detect whether certain rooms are in use. It also monitors and stores data from motion sensors that let it work out whether anyone is home. Then it collects data whenever the user directly interacts with it, by adjusting the temperature. The thermostat uses this knowledge to build an understanding of its users' habits to come up with a schedule to keep them comfortable.

Additionally, the Nest Protect smoke and carbon monoxide sensor detects smoke and $CO_2$ levels. It uses these to raise the alarm when necessary, and can also interact with the thermostat to cut it off in the event of a fire.

The Nest camera records and stores (for up to 30 days depending on the user's subscription level) visual and audio data, which it analyses in real time to provide security. For example, it can send an intruder alert warning to your phone if it detects movement when the house should be empty.

## What Are The Technical Details?

The various Nest devices are built around the company's own proprietary operating system, which is derived from open-source OS Linux as well as a number of other open-source technologies. These devices also use their own wireless communications protocols to talk to each other independently of existing home or workplace wireless network infrastructure. Nest have also developed the Works With Nest protocol, which allows third-party IoT devices including, so far, washing machines, smart wall plugs, fitness tracker bands and smart watches to interface with the devices.

## Any Challenges That Had To Be Overcome?

Privacy is a huge concern, and particularly privacy in the home. I recently spoke to Nest's general manager for Europe, Lionel Paillet, and he was keen to stress how vital it is to his business model to ensure customers' privacy is protected.

He tells me: "Trust is absolutely fundamental to everything we do – particularly in the home, which is sacred, psychologically – it is probably the place that is most private to you on Earth.

"So the notion of user trust has been a guiding principle in everything we have done. Our privacy policy is central to the whole customer experience – it's written on the box, written in the app.

"It's about doing more than giving customers 30 pages of terms and conditions which we know they won't read, and asking them to go to the bottom and tick a box which says they accept."

Google's acquisition of Nest initially sparked fears over what they would do with very sensitive data, such as people's behaviour in their own homes. In particular, this data, many said, would be extremely valuable to insurers and energy companies, which would have real-time access to detailed data on our day-to-day activities. Nest have since stated in no uncertain terms that they will not, under any circumstances, share personal data from the monitors in the thermostats and smoke alarms with anyone, even their parent company. Sceptics, however, have in turn pointed out that this decision may no longer be theirs to make following their acquisition. In addition, with many customers receiving their devices for free or at subsidized rates through power companies (as explained above), there are questions over whether those companies (which may ask customers' permission to monitor their data themselves, as part of their user agreement) will always protect their data with the same rigorousness.

## What Are The Key Learning Points And Takeaways?

Home automation has been a geeky hobby for some time now, but products such as Nest's thermostat mark the emergence of the technology into the mainstream.

However, as Paillet tells me, we shouldn't have *The Jetsons* in mind when we picture the home of the near future – that concept is out of date, before it even came to be.

"What we are interested in is the 'thoughtful home'. Yesterday I used a switch to operate devices in my home. Today I can use my smartphone. But does that really make my life any better?

"The home has to be thoughtful and understand your habits."

Google, Nest's parent company, have long been keen to embed themselves more deeply in both the energy industry (e.g. previous products such a Google Energysense and PowerMeter) as well as our homes. The idea of having a "home computer" is already becoming redundant: why would we need a dedicated device for crunching data and communicating digitally when everything is capable of doing it? It will still need platforms from which we can launch its search engines and operating systems (as well as receive adverts), however. So what makes more sense than a "home operating system" to pin together all these separate pieces of technology?

Paillet tells me: "There was a joke going round when we were first bought, where people were saying they were expecting to start seeing adverts on their thermostats. By now I think everyone has realized that isn't going to happen."

Well, perhaps not our thermostats – but once Google have taken control of their homes, there will be plenty of other places they could find to put them!

## REFERENCES AND FURTHER READING

1. Olson, P. (2014) Nest gives Google its next big data play, http://www.forbes.com/sites/parmyolson/2014/01/13/nest-gives-google-its-next-big-data-play-energy/, accessed 5 January 2016.

2. Patel, N. (2014) Nest CEO Tony Fadell on Google acquisition: "I don't want to retire. I want to build this vision", http://www.theverge.com/2014/1/13/5305430/interview-tony-fadell-nest-google-acquisition, accessed 5 January 2016.

3. Nest Labs (2015) Energy savings from the Nest Learning Thermostat: Energy bill analysis results, https://nest.com/downloads/press/documents/energy-savings-white-paper.pdf, accessed 5 January 2016.

# 19
# GE

*How Big Data Is Fuelling The Industrial Internet*

## Background

GE were born out of Thomas Edison's revolutionary inventions in the latter half of the 19th century which brought electric lighting and machinery into homes and businesses for the first time. They were the first privately owned company to invest in computer hardware and have remained at the forefront of innovation for over a century. Today, their machinery is used in the generation of a quarter of the world's electricity supply.

During the Big Data era, GE – a colossus of a company which generated revenue of almost $150 billion in 2014 and employ over 300,000 staff across their many subsidiaries – have unveiled plans to create what they call the Industrial Internet.

Parallel to the encroachment of smart, digital, connected technology into our everyday lives (smartphones, wearables, even smart light bulbs that Edison himself would be proud of!) a similar movement has been taking place in industry. In manufacturing, transport, finance and aviation, machines are being programmed to talk to each other and communicate in the name of increased productivity and efficiency. GE's Industrial Internet concept has provided much of the groundwork for this transformation. As part of this plan, in 2012 GE announced they would invest $1 billion over four years in their state-of-the-art analytics headquarters in San Ramon, California.

GE's machinery and systems are used in aviation, manufacturing, healthcare, energy production and distribution, mining, water, transportation and finance.

## What Problem Is Big Data Helping To Solve?

When you are operating on the scale of jet engines or power plants, any minor variation in operating efficiency can have dramatic effects on running costs, as well as safety implications.

Downtime of essential machinery can directly lead to loss of revenue, and costly human resources have to be assigned to the upkeep and maintenance of systems.

## How Is Big Data Used In Practice?

Data collected by sensors installed in machinery across every sector in which GE work is measured and analysed to provide information on how it is operating. This means that the effect of minor changes – for example operating temperatures or fuel levels – can be monitored closely, and the effect of altering them correlated with any other metric which is collected.

GE's power turbines, hospital scanners and aircraft engines all constantly monitor the conditions they are operating in, in some cases making the data available in real time or otherwise storing it for later analysis.

For example, in aviation, the data is used to automatically schedule maintenance and reduce delays or workshop congestion caused by unexpected maintenance jobs. The system is able to predict when parts are likely to fail and book engines in for repairs, as well as making sure the workshop will be stocked with the necessary replacement parts. Etihad Airways in Abu Dhabi recently became the first airline to deploy GE's Intelligent Operations technology, developed in partnership with consultants at Accenture.

Of course, it isn't all about burning up the earth's resources as profitably as possible. GE also manufacture and run renewable energy operations. Each of their 22,000 wind turbines situated around the world is monitored and constantly streaming operational data to the cloud, where GE analysts can fine-tune the pitch and direction of the blades to ensure as much energy is being captured as possible. Intelligent learning algorithms allow each individual turbine to adapt its behaviour to mimic other nearby turbines which are operating more efficiently.

These Industrial Internet capabilities are being made available to GE's customers who operate their equipment and systems as part of their business: power companies, airlines, banks, hospitals and countless others. They can upload their own usage data to the Hadoop-powered distributed cloud network, where it can be analysed using their proprietary GE Predictivity analytics systems as well as software developed with other partners, and open-source solutions.

## What Were The Results?

Although GE have not released overall figures, they have said that their industrial customers can expect to save an average of $8 million per year from the reduction in machine downtime alone.

They have also said that if their systems can improve operating efficiency across five of their key sectors then businesses adopting their Big Data-driven technology can expect to make combined savings of $300 billion. Analytics in general, GE CEO Jeff Immelt has claimed, could create between $10 trillion and $15 trillion value in the world economy over the next 20 years.

## What Data Was Used?

GE generate, capture and analyse internal data from the operation of their machines, as well as external data from a wide range of outside suppliers including meteorological, geopolitical and demographic data.

This external data includes satellite imagery. One use that GE find for this is working out where vegetation should be cut back to avoid the risk of power cuts caused by falling trees during storms.

Just one of their gas power station turbines generates around 500 gigabytes a day, covering everything from the environmental temperature it is operating at to its efficiency at converting burning coal into electrical energy.

## What Are The Technical Details?

In 2013, Immelt said that Industrial Internet sensors had already been installed in 250,000 pieces of machinery distributed around the world. All of this data is fed into their Hadoop-based Industrial Data Lake service, which customers can "plug in" to and access data that is relevant to their industry as quickly as possible, often in real time. It provides a range of tools to access and interpret this data, including its own Predictivity and Predix services, as well as tools developed with partners such as Pivotal and Accenture.

## Any Challenges That Had To Be Overcome?

The largest challenge facing GE's systems architects and engineers while rolling out their Industrial Internet infrastructure was scale. The sheer number of industries their machinery operates in, and the spread of customers around the world, meant that creating systems which would be valuable to all of them while centralizing the storage and analytics of data was a huge task.

GE met the challenge by vastly increasing their investment in analytics staff and research in order to be able to cope with meeting the demand for services capable of carrying out high-speed analytics on large data volumes. It established their analytics operations in the Bay Area of San Francisco to take advantage of the talent there. This also gave GE exposure to startups working on analytics-led technology, which they partnered with and in some cases invested in or acquired. This rapid expansion of analytics resources and capabilities was necessary to meet the growing demand from GE's industrial customers.

## What Are The Key Learning Points And Takeaways?

GE have responded with remarkable speed and agility to the arrival of Big Data and the IoT in the worlds of business and industry. By seeing the value of adopting advanced analytics technology at an early stage in the game, they have continued to act in the pioneering manner in which they first built their name.

Interconnected technology has vast potential for improving efficiency across all sectors. Why wait for machines to go wrong or fail when it could be predicted and downtime kept to a minimum? Machines are capable of making such predictions far more reliably than people are, so it makes perfect sense to teach them how to do it.

GE have shown that data combined with analytics is the key to driving these efficiencies.

### REFERENCES AND FURTHER READING

For more information on GE's use of data see:

http://files.gereports.com/wp-content/uploads/2012/11/ge-industrial-internet-vision-paper.pdf

http://www.infoworld.com/article/2616433/big-data/general-electric-lays-out-big-plans-for-big-data.html

http://sites.tcs.com/big-data-study/ge-big-data-case-study/

# 20
# ETSY

*How Big Data Is Used In A Crafty Way*

## Background

Etsy, the online marketplace which connects sellers of handmade and vintage products with buyers from around the world, was founded in 2005 in a New York apartment. Over the past decade, it has risen to become a leader in the market for peer-to-peer trading, enabling small-scale manufacturers and retailers to make millions of sales each month. All of this has been achieved by optimizing and streamlining the process of both buying and selling, to provide users, regardless of how tech-savvy they are, with the most comfortable experience.

## What Problem Is Big Data Helping To Solve?

Sellers range from professional craftspeople to hobbyists, many of them operating their business as a sideline in addition to their full-time income. Its success at attracting so many is down to its simplicity – anyone can sign up for an account and start selling immediately. This form of peer-to-peer trading also takes place on sites geared to more commercial retailing, for example Amazon and eBay. But Etsy has built a name as the place to look for "individual" or "unique" items, which are often given as gifts. With over 32 million unique items available on the site, helping customers find just what they're looking for – whether it's a handmade baby blanket or a moustache mug – is the big challenge.

Speaking to the *Wall Street Journal,* John Allspaw, Etsy's senior vice president for infrastructure and operations explained: "Because of the uniqueness, we have to do a lot more work to figure out what you're looking for … Building personalization and recommendations is a much harder problem because we have to look for deeper signals."

## How Is Big Data Used In Practice?

Despite the traditional nature of many of the crafts and items on offer, state-of-the-art Big Data technology beats at the heart of the business, and has been key to Etsy's success at evolving into a global brand. By monitoring and analysing every click made by visitors and customers to their site, their data engineers are able to analyse what behaviour leads to a sale, and what leads to customers leaving the site, unable to find what they are looking for. By monitoring users' behaviour on the site, Etsy are able to provide personalized recommendations and search results in real time.

In another example of data-based insight, the company noticed that, while relatively few people were using a bookmark button to mark favourite products, those who did were more likely to sign up for an account on the site. By simply increasing the prominence of this button on the page, an immediate increase in signups was noticed.

Analytics is inbuilt into every department in the company – not confined to marketing, as with many businesses. This is made possible by the company's internal processes, which allow any of their engineers to deploy test code in real time in order to carry out experiments and record their impact on KPIs. In their own words, this is like "changing the tyres without stopping the car".

It has been reported that 20 to 30 updates to the site are made in this way each day. Every week, 80% of the company's total workforce access data that is stored in their data centres. In 2009, the company acquired Adtuitive, a delivery platform for targeted online retail advertising, and incorporated their servers and algorithms with their own.

It is a sign of how seriously Etsy take Big Data that their current CEO, Chad Dickerson, was formerly CTO of the company, and designed much of the business's data-driven marketing strategy. Much like their competitors, which sell more mainstream, mass-produced goods, they have built their own recommendation engine, which suggests what products visitors may be interested in browsing.

Big Data analytical routines are also deployed for fraud prevention – scanning the thousands of transactions that take place across their servers every day for telltale signs of dishonest activity.

## What Were The Results?

Etsy's reported revenue continues to rise, even if the company's share price has taken a hit since their IPO in April 2015. For the first half of 2015, Etsy reported total revenue of $119 million, up 44% on the same period in 2014.

In ten years, Etsy have successfully leveraged the Internet as a marketplace for bespoke, handcrafted or homemade goods. With 21.7 million active buyers and a community of 1.5 million active sellers, Etsy is the go-to place for unique products and gifts. None of this would have been possible without their keen embracing of Big Data and analytics.

## What Data Was Used?

Both transactional (sales) and behavioural (browsing) data are collected. Etsy generate a huge amount of clickstream data, including how users move around the site and how long they linger on a product. This transactional and browsing data is shared with the sellers themselves through their Shop Stats system, allowing them to carry out their own analysis and hopefully increase their own revenues – and, of course, Etsy's share of the sale.

## What Are The Technical Details?

All of the company's data is collected on a Hadoop framework, run in-house as opposed to in the cloud. (Etsy started off with Amazon's cloud-based Elastic MapReduce service but decided to bring everything in-house after a year.) Apache Kafka helps Etsy stay on top of their data pipeline and load data into Hadoop. On top of this, Etsy operate an open-source, machine-learning framework called Conjecture that helps create the predictive models which power user recommendations and search results in real time. While Hadoop is ideal for Etsy's large-scale data mining, the company also use an SQL engine on top of Hadoop for more ad hoc data queries.

## Any Challenges That Had To Be Overcome?

Etsy are keen to foster an environment of Big Data innovation and experimentation, but that requires broad access to and wide utilization of data across the company. Etsy found this difficult to achieve until the data was brought in-house. Speaking to TechRepublic, Etsy's CTO Kellan Elliott-McCrea explained that bringing it in-house resulted in a tenfold increase in utilization of the data (as mentioned before, 80% of the workforce now access and use this data on a weekly basis). Contrary to the common assumption that the cloud encourages greater experimentation with data, Elliot-McCrea argues: "You can get better experimentation – assuming you have the experience running a data centre – if you bring it in-house."

There are likely to be new challenges for Etsy as the artisan marketplace gets more competitive. Amazon are reported to be launching a rival service called Amazon Handmade. Amazon's already skilful use of Big Data will no doubt make them a very tough competitor.

# What Are The Key Learning Points And Takeaways?

Two things jump out at me in Etsy's use of Big Data. The first is their wide adoption of data across the whole company. It's hard to think of many other retail companies where 80% of their staff are using data on a weekly basis to drive their decision making. But Etsy show how this is achievable and desirable. Second, it's clear that creating a personalized experience for customers is of utmost important to Etsy, and this is something all retailers can learn from. But, as Allspaw says: "There is generating real-time recommendations for buyers and then there is generating real-time recommendations for buyers that are actually good."[1]

## REFERENCES AND FURTHER READING

1. WSJ (2015) Etsy Leans on Machine Learning to Help You Find Just the Right Bedazzled Wallet http://blogs.wsj.com/cio/2015/06/05/etsy-leans-on-machine-learning-to-help-you-find-just-the-right-bedazzled-wallet/, accessed 5 January 2016.

You can find out more about Etsy and Big Data in these articles:

http://www.techrepublic.com/article/etsy-goes-retro-to-scale/

https://channels.theinnovationenterprise.com/presentations/big-data-at-etsy

# 21
# NARRATIVE SCIENCE
*How Big Data Is Used To Tell Stories*

## Background

As humans, we have always found stories a useful medium for passing on information. This includes truthful accounts meant to educate us, fictional stories meant to entertain us and the whole spectrum in between.

Narrative Science are a Chicago company which have taken up the challenge of automating that process using Big Data. They began by publishing automated reports of sports games for the Big 10 network and have evolved to produce business and financial news for international media organizations such as Forbes.

They do this through a process known as Natural Language Generation – using sophisticated machine-learning procedures to craft facts and figures from computer databases into stories that appear to have been written by humans.

## What Problem Is Big Data Helping To Solve?

The human brain can easily overload itself on information and get lost in huge tables of charts and figures. A tragic example of this involves the 1986 Space Shuttle *Challenger* disaster. Mission controllers were passed an overwhelming amount of information from the technical staff monitoring the shuttle's vital systems. Undoubtedly, hidden somewhere amongst that information would have been clues that could have told them the shuttle was going to explode. However, owing to their being buried in countless charts, diagrams and reams of printed figures, the warning signs weren't spotted – with disastrous consequences.

In addition, sometimes the same data will mean different things to different people. Those with responsibility for reporting findings of data-driven investigations have the task of transforming charts and statistics into actionable insights, in a way that can be clearly understood by those who will have to put them into action. This takes time, effort and most vitally a special level of communications ability on the part of the person doing the reporting.

In the media world, a journalist interpreting complicated financial, technical or legal data for the benefit of a lay audience requires the same skillset. The journalist's – or any storyteller's – job is to point out to the reader what is "wood" and what is "trees", to inform them of the relevance of the information being reported. In other words, they have to make the reader aware of how the events being reported are likely to affect their own lives.

This means the readers or viewers of a report have to have faith in the people who put it together – fallible humans – that they will correctly discern the relevant information themselves, and pass it on in an accurate and unbiased way. Anyone who has ever read a newspaper will know that this isn't always what happens in practice!

## How Is Big Data Used In Practice?

Narrative Science have created Quill$^{TM}$ – which they refer to as a "natural language generation platform". Quill$^{TM}$ takes information from charts and statistics which are fed into it and turns them into "stories" – narratives written in plain English and targeted at those who are in a position to put the information they contain to use.

These stories are used as news reports by media outlets, as well as to create industry-specific reports and by individual companies for their own internal communications.

Clients include Forbes, MasterCard and the UK National Health Service. All of these access Quill™ through a software-as-a-service (SAAS), cloud-based platform which allows them to feed in the specific information relevant to their intended audiences, and output reports written in easily digestible, natural human language.

## What Were The Results?

The result is written copy which is practically unidentifiable from that created by human authors. Major media organizations, including Forbes, have been using the software to create news pieces for several years – the results are archived on their website[1] and here are a couple of samples:

> Analysts expect higher profit for DTE Energy when the company reports its second quarter results on Friday, July 24, 2015. The consensus estimate is calling for profit of 84 cents a share, reflecting a rise from 73 cents per share a year ago.

> Analysts expect decreased profit for Fidelity National Information Services when the company reports its second quarter results on Thursday, July 23, 2015. Although Fidelity National Information reported profit of 75 cents a year ago, the consensus estimate calls for earnings per share of 71 cents.

Pretty good, I would say, and I don't think I would recognize that it wasn't written by a human if I didn't know before I read it!

# What Data Was Used?

The Quill$^{TM}$ system ingests structured data, fed to it in formats such as JSON, XML, CSV, etc. Initially, Narrative Science took data compiled during sports games and turned them into reports for the Big 10 Network.

The company quickly realized it had far wider potential applications – founder Kris Hammond tells me: "We very early on realized the technology could solve what was clearly a very pressing problem: the understanding and interpretation of analytics.

"The numbers don't do it, visualizations and dashboards don't do it. We were taking people with really high-class talent and having them sit down in front of screens and write things up for people who were very smart but did not have analytical skills.

"We realized that was something that Quill$^{TM}$ can do – it can cover the last mile, and be the thing that explains everything else. We essentially became a B2B business."

Since then other uses have been found for Quill$^{TM}$, including in real estate, where property sales data and economic activity data can be transformed into reports for home buyers or investors, financial data which can be compiled into market reports for financiers and fund managers and government data which can be transformed into action points for those who provide public services.

The free Quill Engage$^{TM}$ service creates custom reports for website owners using data taken from Google Analytics.

# What Are The Technical Details?

The data is crunched using its cloud-based SAAS platform. The database is hosed in the Amazon Web Services (AWS) cloud. The data is then analysed and transformed into narratives using artificial intelligence algorithms. In particular, the company applies NLG (natural language generation), which is a subfield of artificial intelligence. Narrative Science have patented the technology, which brings together data analytics, reasoning and narrative generation.

## Any Challenges That Had To Be Overcome?

Natural language generation presents significant problems, mainly owing to the many different ways in which we communicate, and the subtle nuances in language. Although Quill™ currently only operates in English, there are many different varieties and dialects of English, often using the same words but very different patterns and semantic structure to put them together.

This was solved by putting a great deal of emphasis on the underlying structure that gives context and meaning to a collection of words.

As Kris Hammond says: "Even before you get to the point where you're saying 'here's the language', the system looks at the data and considers some crucial things – how would it characterize what is going on here, what is important and what is interesting?

"All of this goes into play before the language ever shows up. Language is, even for us, the last mile. The structure of the story and narrative comes first."

## What Are The Key Learning Points And Takeaways?

Reporting the most essential and valuable insights your data contains is a vital part of the analytic process and requires specialized communications skills – both in humans and in machines.

Computers are increasingly becoming competent at tasks which we previously would have thought were better suited to humans, for example creating reports and stories in natural, written language.

There are still some areas of communication where humans are ahead of computers: while they are getting better at reporting, they still aren't able to find stories of their own to report. Quill$^{TM}$ relies on the program being fed the necessary data rather than being able to hunt it down itself. This will undoubtedly be an area of further research for natural language generation in the near future.

## REFERENCES AND FURTHER READING
1. Articles for Forbes created using Quill's$^{TM}$ natural language generation can be found at: http://www.forbes.com/sites/narrativescience/

# 22
# BBC

*How Big Data Is Used In The Media*

## Background

The BBC (British Broadcasting Corporation) are one of the world's largest media organizations and, as a public service broadcaster, have a relatively unique remit to operate without funding from advertisers.

This stipulation in their charter is designed to enable them to operate free of corporate interference. However, their licence-fee-based structure also gives them some freedom to innovate, as risks can be taken when commissioning programming when you don't have to worry about attracting big advertising bucks.

Where they do not differ from most other large media organizations, however, is in their wide-scale adoption of Big Data and analytics technology. As a large proportion of the BBC's output is now digital, through their iPlayer and BBC Online services, they are generating and collecting ever-increasing amounts of data and using it to tailor output to their audience.

## What Problem Is Big Data Helping To Solve?

In their native market, the BBC have a remit to produce content that will be of value – defined as content which either "educates, informs or entertains" by John Reith, the corporation's first director general.

Internationally, they operate a little differently, through their BBC Worldwide arm, which uses advertising to generate revenue, and in this market they compete with private-sector broadcasters and news media.

This means that the problem facing the BBC is fundamentally the same: how to produce content that will attract an audience, by providing them with value.

Digital content is generally not presented in a linear fashion – as with scheduled TV, radio or traditional newspapers – but effectively gives the audience the ability to produce their own schedules by choosing what they want to read, watch or listen to next.

This means the audience's attention has to be fought for at every turn – unlike in the old days, where it was known that attracting a viewer at the start of peak viewing time with a star show would mean it was likely you would have their attention for the rest of the evening.

## How Is Big Data Used In Practice?

The BBC are renowned throughout the world for their news reporting, and using data analytics to improve the depth, breadth and presentation of their journalism has been a key part of the BBC's Big Data strategy.

In 2013, the BBC advertised for partners on Big Data projects, putting £18 million on the table for businesses to help them develop platforms and frameworks for analytics and predictive modelling. In particular, they were looking for help with algorithmic content recommendations – suggesting which TV programmes or news reports, individuals should consume next – and social media analytics.

One initiative, known as myBBC, was aimed at investigating and deepening the corporation's relationship with their audience, through developing more relevant content for the Web portal BBC Online, encouraging greater volumes of two-way communication through social media and providing insights that could clue editorial and creative teams in on what viewers wanted to see more of.

They have also experimented with facial-recognition technology to gauge audience's responses to TV programming during trials.[1] The corporation's Preview Screen Lab monitored the reaction of viewers of 50 different shows in four countries, using cameras designed to monitor audience members' faces and interpret the emotions being displayed. In one experiment, a number of households in Australia were monitored to capture the reactions of the audience as they watched a trailer for a season premiere of the show *Sherlock*.

## What Were The Results?

The results of the trial in Australia were that researchers discovered viewers who went on to rate the show highly showed a greater reaction to events on screen that were tagged as "surprising" or "sad", rather than "funny". This led the programme's producers to include more dark, thriller elements in the show in favour of less comedy.

## What Data Was Used?

The BBC collect data on when and how their digital output is viewed through the iPlayer service. Information on usage of the BBC Online Web portal is also collected and monitored. This is augmented with demographic information that is collected either from the user when signing up to services or from public records. They also use social media analysis to gauge audience response to their programme output. The Preview Screen Lab project captures facial expressions from the audiences that it is monitoring.

## What Are The Technical Details?

Journalists at the BBC's online news arm are all trained in basic data analytical skills, involving the use of Excel and Google Fusion tables to interrogate data and turn it into stories.

For larger datasets, analysts rely on technologies including MySQL and Apache Solr. The journalism team include people whose primary skill is in software development, and these tend to specialize in programming languages suited to data science, such as R and Python.

## Any Challenges That Had To Be Overcome?

As a public service broadcaster, directly accountable to both Government and the taxpayer, the BBC have acknowledged that they need to take a more conservative approach to privacy and data protection than is generally displayed by private-sector media organizations.

Michael Fleshman, head of consumer digital technology at BBC Worldwide, told Web magazine *Computing*: "[The] BBC as a whole takes a very conservative approach. There are intensive checkpoints organizationally and process-wise to make certain we are taking that conservative approach."[2]

Reportedly, the overarching principle at the BBC regarding Big Data projects is that if there are concerns privacy or data protection may be put at risk a project will not be put into action.

Another challenge faced by the BBC is that of scalability. Because of the unique way in which the corporation are funded, they aren't allowed to display advertising on their UK services, where the majority of their output is consumed. This means a huge spike in visitor numbers for a particular piece of content – say a very popular news report – does not come with the accompanying spike in ad revenue a commercial service would expect. It does, however, still entail the accompanying spike in bandwidth costs. As BBC chief technical architect Dirk-Willem Van Gulik told *Macworld* in 2011: "Our income stays the same, we don't get a penny more.

"So when we get ten times as many users we have to figure out a way to do things ten times cheaper."[3]

Because of this, the technical infrastructure used to run the BBC's data operation was developed on the principle that it should be as cost efficient as possible. Measures included building their own servers to reduce the reliance on off-the-shelf solutions and using tape media for storage rather than hard drives, which are more expensive and fail more regularly, leading to higher maintenance costs.

## What Are The Key Learning Points And Takeaways?

The digital environments in which modern media companies operate mean they are ideally situated to take advantage of the growing use of Big Data technology. This applies whether they are publicly or privately funded – either way the aim is to grow audience share by providing content of greater value to consumers than the competition is.

The BBC have some advantages – such as the lack of need to keep advertisers happy – which in some ways means they are freer to innovate without the constant necessity of proving that their innovation will affect the corporation's bottom line.

However, they also face unique challenges, including the greater need to take data privacy and security seriously. As they are accountable to the public through the licence fee they pay and ultimately Parliament, breaches or slip-ups in this area could have political ramifications and are unlikely to be tolerated.

## REFERENCES AND FURTHER READING

1. WSJ (2015) BBC facial recognition software analyzes audience response, http://blogs.wsj.com/cio/2015/05/29/bbc-facial-recognition-software-analyzes-audience-response/, accessed 5 January 2016.

2. Palmer, D. (2014) BBC's conservative approach to data makes our jobs a little harder, http://www.computing.co.uk/ctg/news/2379410/bbcs-conservative-approach-to-data-use-makes-our-jobs-a-little-harder, accessed 5 January 2016.

3. Essers, L. (2011) BBC tackles Big Data Dilemma with smart IT structuring, http://www.macworld.co.uk/news/apple/bbc-tackles-big-data-dilemma-smart-it-structuring-3288278/, accessed 5 January 2016.

For more information on data in journalism visit:

http://datajournalismhandbook.org/1.0/en/in_the_newsroom_1.html

# 23
# MILTON KEYNES

*How Big Data Is Used To Create Smarter Cities*

## Background

Milton Keynes is a large town (technically – although it is often referred to as a city) in the middle of England with a population of around 230,000. It is a "new town" developed in the Sixties and designed to house the ever-growing London overspill population. From the start it was developed with telecommunications in mind – following a grid pattern based on modern American city planning techniques, and without the traditional "town centre" from which traditional, organically grown cities and towns had naturally evolved.

The idea was that telecommunications would do away with the need for citizens to commute in large numbers into town centres to work, where businesses would be grouped closely together, before returning home to the suburbs in the evenings. Telephones meant businesses could trade without having to meet face-to-face in the local market. This gave rise to out-of-town warehousing and logistics sites on cheaper, undeveloped land with good access to transport infrastructure such as motorways.

By the early 2000s, this idea was still evolving, and the rapid expansion of Internet communications gave rise to the concept of the "smart city". This involves applying technology, including IT and Big Data principles, to every area of civic life, from waste management to public transport, with the aim of improving the quality of life for the people living there.

Thanks to its great links to other major cities such as London and Birmingham, by this time Milton Keynes had grown into a tech hub in its own right, with a young and technically inclined population. This meant it was a natural choice for a UK smart city project.

To this end, the city council applied for, and were eventually awarded, a £16 million grant from the Government and BT, with the aim of kick-starting development of smart city infrastructure projects in Milton Keynes.

## What Problem Is Big Data Helping To Solve?

In line with growth forecasts for other cities in the UK and around the world, the population of Milton Keynes is expected to continue to quickly grow in coming years. Estimates say a further 50,000 people will call it home in 10 years' time, swelling the population to around 350,000.

Existing civic infrastructure will be hard pressed to deal with this. Roads are at risk of becoming congested, current public transport facilities will be insufficient, air quality will be reduced, waste facilities will overflow and schools will be overcrowded. All of these will inevitably lead to a decline in the quality of life for the people living there.

On top of this, all cities in the UK and much of the developed world have committed to reducing the amount of carbon emissions released into the air, in order to mitigate the effects of climate change.

# How Is Big Data Used In Practice?

Around three years ago, Milton Keynes' council could see the value of a data-driven approach to infrastructure planning and service delivery but lacked the in-house skills to implement the technology. They approached the business community for assistance and, after establishing a series of forums for discussing possible options for the future, began working with several partners to develop the vision of Smart City Milton Keynes.

One key initiative, developed with the help of the Open University and BT, is MK: Smart.[1] It will act as a data hub for all of the other projects in the city where their effectiveness and impact can be assessed.

Internet of Things (IoT) type, connected solutions have been proposed for transport, energy efficiency, water supply planning, enterprise growth and provision of education. Sensors will be installed at waste disposal facilities, meaning the process of emptying them by truck can be made more efficient. Traffic and footfall through public spaces will also be monitored in order to plan public transport routes as well as footpath and cycle path infrastructure.

Many of the projects are underway, with a number of homes taking part in trials of energy-saving home appliances and smart meters, in association with energy provider E.ON. Other families have been provided with free electric cars in order to carry out a year-long viability study on the technology. And in the near future, the city will see the first UK trials of driverless cars on its grid-like, roundabout-heavy road network.

The latest initiative, CAPE, uses satellite imagery and data on thermal leakage of houses; the aim is to help citizens to manage their own community energy schemes and ultimately reduce their carbon footprint. It will supplement satellite imagery with building and energy data to locate neighbourhoods that could benefit from an energy makeover. It's a first in the UK and the latest addition to the MK: Smart programme.

## What Were The Results?

Although the project is in its early stages, Milton Keynes' council are already working with over 40 partners on projects across the city.

Geoff Snelson, director of strategy at the council, tells me the theory and technology have been proved and that the emphasis is now on developing sustainable business cases for developing and delivering the services.

He says: "Internationally, there is a real dearth of hard evidence about the benefits that these bring, and we are trying to correct that.

"We've got a lot of research and development funding, but now we are moving to the stage where we are pushing into the development of real commercial models.

"A lot of these solutions are about delivering efficiencies by gathering better – more timely and more accurate – information. It's not voodoo – just better information. It's not really about proving the tech works any more. It's about proving that it works in a sustainable way in a real urban environment."

## What Data Was Used?

Satellite images overlaid with planning guidelines data are used to monitor the growth of "urban sprawl" and ensure that building development is taking place in line with strategy and regulations.

Data is collected from more than 80 council-run refuse disposal sites, to ensure they are being emptied in an optimal way – cutting down on wasted journeys and unnecessary $CO_2$ emissions.

Sensors monitor the flow of traffic on roads through the city, which is used to alert motorists to congestion and plan future infrastructure development.

Smart street lighting technology gathers data on when and where people are walking at night-time, to ensure illumination where necessary for safety and energy conservation where not.

Data on water and energy usage is gathered to better understand demand and to help plan for supply.

Social media use in the city is analysed for sentiment towards the projects in use and under development. In addition, social media use in other areas is monitored, to compare how well the civic authorities communicate with their citizens compared to in other cities and towns around the UK.

## What Are The Technical Details?

An analytics platform designed by the Indian company Tech Mahindra, which have an office in the town, provides much of the data processing infrastructure of MK: Smart.

The Tech Mahindra Analytics Platform is based on Hadoop. Other open-source technologies – including Sqoop, Flume, Spark, Oozie, Mahout and Hive – are also extensively used. Current use cases typically involve around 600 gigabytes to 1 terabyte of data, with daily queries numbering in the hundreds of thousands; however, the system has been designed to handle much larger use cases that could emerge in the near future.

## Any Challenges That Had To Be Overcome?

Because of the lack of specialist knowledge of technology and data analysis within the council, partnerships with other organizations were developed.

One which is playing a key part in the development of MK: Smart is Tech Mahindra, mentioned above, that have had a presence in Milton Keynes since the turn of the century.

Their vice president of global transformation, Upendra Dharmadhkary, tells me: "We had been doing emergency response management in India, where there is 10 times the population, and we thought, 'Why can't we apply some of the technology here?'

"We have frequent discussions with the council and a good working relationship. I think the council is one of the few in the UK which is agile enough to think about and implement these ideas."

Another potential concern was how the public would react to the encroachment of technology into their everyday lives, particularly elements such as the driverless cars, which, although theoretically far safer than human-controlled cars, are largely untested.

Geoff Snelson tells me: "They do need to be introduced quite carefully. Of course, there are safety considerations – but in Milton Keynes people are generally quite excited about it – they take pride in it even.

"There's quite an appetite for things that position Milton Keynes as an exciting and interesting place."

## What Are The Key Learning Points And Takeaways?

City populations around the world are booming – smart, connected IoT technologies will be necessary now and in the future to allow infrastructure development to keep up.

IoT and smart city tech have the potential to hugely improve efficiency in the delivery of public services, and make cities more pleasant to live in.

Although investment in these areas must have a provable business case, as funding budgets are limited, particularly so in times of economic recession or depression, "thinking smart" about infrastructure development, while incurring short-term costs, may provide long-term savings.

## REFERENCES AND FURTHER READING
1. http://www.mksmart.org/

For more information on smart cities visit:

http://www.uoc.edu/uocpapers/5/dt/eng/mitchell.pdf

# 24
# PALANTIR

*How Big Data Is Used To Help The CIA And To Detect Bombs In Afghanistan*

## Background

Palantir, named after the magical stones in *The Lord of The Rings* used for spying, have made a name for themselves using Big Data to solve security problems ranging from fraud to terrorism. Their systems were developed with funding from the CIA and are widely used by the US Government and their security agencies. Their annual revenue is reported to be in the region of $500 million and they are forecasted to grow even larger – at the time of writing (January 2016) the company are tipped to go public with an IPO and are currently valued at $20 billion.

## What Problem Is Big Data Helping To Solve?

Initially working on tools to spot fraudulent transactions made with credit cards, Palantir soon realized the same pattern-analysis methods could work for disrupting all forms of criminal activity, from terrorism to the international drug trade. Now, their sophisticated Big Data analytics technology is being used to crack down on crime and terrorism.

# How Is Big Data Used In Practice?

Palantir build platforms that integrate and manage huge datasets, which can then be analysed by their wide range of clients – including government agencies and the financial and pharmaceutical industries.

Much of their work is naturally veiled in secrecy, but it is widely known that their routines for spotting patterns and anomalies in data which indicate suspicious or fraudulent activity are derived from technology developed by PayPal (Peter Thiel, who also co-founded the online payment service, is a Palantir co-founder).

They have been credited with revealing trends that have helped deal with the threat of IEDs (improvised explosive devices), suicide bombers in Syria and Pakistan and even infiltration of allied governments by spies. The US Government are Palantir's biggest customer, and their software has become one of the most effective weapons in the digital front of the "war on terror". Marines, for example, have used Palantir tools to analyse roadside bombs in Afghanistan and predict attacks and the placement of bombs.

The data needed to support Marines in Afghanistan was often spread across many sources without one single interface to access and analyse the data. Therefore, the United States Marine Corps (USMC) charged Palantir with developing a system that could integrate these sources quickly. The aim was to improve overall intelligence and reduce the amount of time spent looking for information. As units are often working in areas with low bandwidth or with no bandwidth at all, the system had to work without being connected to base stations. The Palantir Forward system provided the answer to this problem, as it automatically synchronized data whenever the connection to base stations was restored. USMC analysts were able to use Palantir's data integration, search, discovery and analytic technology to fuse the data and provide greater intelligence to Marines on the frontline.

A key philosophy of the company is that human intervention is still needed to get the most from data analysis – particularly when you have to think one step ahead of an enemy. To this end, they provide handpicked expert consultants to work in the field alongside their clients on data projects.

## What Were The Results?

Using Palantir's system, USMC analysts were able to detect correlations between weather data and IED attacks, and linked biometric data collected from IEDs to specific individuals and networks. None of this would have been possible without having all the data integrated and synchronized in one place.

Palantir have now raised $1.5 billion in venture capital funding, indicating an enormous level of confidence in their technology. And the power of their platforms is being recognized beyond the realm of law enforcement and defence; the company are attracting many corporate clients, such as Hershey's, who are collaborating with Palantir on a data-sharing group.

## What Data Was Used?

In the Afghanistan example, the data used included a wide range of structured and unstructured data: DNA databases, surveillance records showing movements, social media data, tip-offs from informants, sensor data, geographical data, weather data and biometric data from IEDs. A big part of Palantir's success lies in pulling such massive data sets together effectively.

## What Are The Technical Details?

Palantir are understandably secretive about technical details, which means I am unable to share details on how data is stored or analysed.

## Any Challenges That Had To Be Overcome?

Privacy is a murky area in the Big Data world, and for companies such as Palantir that gather enormous amounts of data public perceptions surrounding their use of that data is bound to be a concern. The company were implicated in the WikiLeaks scandal, when they were named as one of three tech firms approached by lawyers on behalf of Bank of America seeking proposals for dealing with an expected release of sensitive information. After their name was linked to the scandal, Palantir issued an apology for their involvement.

Concerns are growing about government use of individuals' data, particularly in the US and the UK, in the wake of the Edward Snowden NSA leaks. As such, Palantir need to tread a fine line between gathering the data necessary for the job at hand and avoiding mass invasion of privacy. It's an issue that founder Alex Karp doesn't shy away from. Speaking to Forbes a couple of years ago, he said: "I didn't sign up for the government to know when I smoke a joint or have an affair." And in a company address he stated: "We have to find places that we protect away from government so that we can all be the unique and interesting and, in my case, somewhat deviant people we'd like to be."[1] With the company's reported IPO coming up, public perception is likely to be as important as ever and it'll be interesting to see how they manage this.

## What Are The Key Learning Points And Takeaways?

One of the key points that Palantir make is that human interaction with data is just as valuable as the data itself. This is true whether you're fighting a war or trying to attract new customers to your product or service. There is a danger that we place too much blind faith in data itself, when, in fact, how we work with that data and make decisions based on it is the key.

Palantir also provide an excellent example of how data can be especially powerful when more than one dataset is combined. Working with just one dataset can provide a very one-sided view – often it's the correlations and interactions between different types of data that provide the real insight gems.

## REFERENCES AND FURTHER READING

1. Greenberg, A. (2013) How a "deviant" philosopher built Palantir: A Cia-funded data-mining juggernaut, http://www.forbes.com/sites/andy greenberg/2013/08/14/agent-of-intelligence-how-a-deviant-philosopher -built-palantir-a-cia-funded-data-mining-juggernaut/, accessed 5 January 2016.

You can read more about Palantir at:

https://www.palantir.com/

https://www.palantir.com/wp-assets/wp-content/uploads/2014/03/ Impact-Study-Fielding-an-Advanced-Analytic-Capability-in-a-War-Zone.pdf

http://siliconangle.com/blog/2014/12/15/palantir-secures-first-60m-chunk-of-projected-400m-round-as-market-asks-who/

http://moneymorning.com/2015/07/28/as-palantir-ipo-date-approaches-heres-what-investors-need-to-know/

http://www.wsj.com/articles/SB100014240527023034978045792405010 78423362

# 25
# AIRBNB

*How Big Data Is Used To Disrupt The Hospitality Industry*

## Background

Airbnb, the website that connects travellers with available accommodation around the world, launched in 2008. Since then, the company have collected a huge amount of data – around 1.5 petabytes – on people's holiday habits and accommodation preferences.

## What Problem Is Big Data Helping To Solve?

With 1.5 million listings across 34,000 cities, and 50 million guests, Airbnb's biggest challenge is to connect large volumes of guests with those who have accommodation to offer (whether it's a room or a whole apartment/house). Doing this successfully requires an understanding of hosts' and guests' preferences so that the right sort of properties are available in desirable areas at key times – and for the right price.

## How Is Big Data Used In Practice?

Writing on Airbnb's 'Nerds' hub, Riley Newman, head of data science, says: "A datum is a record of an action or event, which in most cases reflects a decision made by a person. If you can recreate the sequence of events leading up to that decision, you can learn from it; it's an indirect way of the person telling you what they like and don't like – this property is more attractive than that one, I find these features useful but those ... not so much. This sort of feedback can be a gold-mine for decisions about community growth, product development and resource prioritization ... we translate the customer's 'voice' into a language more suitable for decision-making."

The insight gained from this feedback enables Airbnb to ensure they concentrate efforts on signing up landlords in popular destinations at peak times, and structure pricing so that the use of their global network of properties is optimized. For example, data is used to determine the appropriate price of a room or apartment, based on a number of variables such as location, time of year, type of accommodation, transport links, etc. Airbnb use an algorithm to help their hosts determine the right price for their offering. This is particularly challenging given the sheer range of accommodation available and when you consider these are real homes, not bog-standard hotel rooms that can be easily rated on a star system. After all, what is desirable in a city apartment (Wi-Fi, good transport links, etc.) may be less important in a quaint cottage (where the guests may prefer peace and romantic decor over Wi-Fi and subway connections).

To help hosts set the price, Airbnb released a machine-learning platform called Aerosolve. The platform analyses images from the host's photos (listings with photos of cosy bedrooms are more successful than those with stylish living rooms!) and automatically divides cities into micro-neighbourhoods. The platform also incorporates dynamic pricing tips that mimic hotel and airline pricing models. In short, Aerosolve's algorithm reflects the insights Airbnb have gained about their customers and how this influences the price of a property. For example, people are willing to pay more if a listing has lots of reviews. All this data is combined into a dashboard that helps hosts determine the best price for their accommodation.

Airbnb have also just unveiled Airpal: a user-friendly data analysis platform designed to allow all of their employees, not just those trained in data science, access to all of the company's information, and tools to query it with.

In addition, proprietary-learning algorithms are in place across the network to predict fraudulent transactions before they are processed, and a robust recommendation system allows guests and hosts to rate each other to build trust.

## What Were The Results?

As Newman says: "Measuring the impact of a data science team is ironically difficult, but one signal is that there's now a unanimous desire to consult data for decisions that need to be made by technical and non-technical people alike." This is demonstrated in the Airpal system; launched in 2014, Airpal has already been used by more than one-third of Airbnb employees to issue queries. This impressive statistic shows how central data has become to Airbnb's decision making.

The growth of Airbnb is another indication that their clever use of data is paying off.

## What Data Was Used?

Data is primarily internal across a mixture of structured and unstructured formats: image data from host photos, location data, accommodation features (number of rooms/beds, Wi-Fi, hot tub, etc.), customer feedback and ratings, transaction data, etc. Some external data is analysed, too, for example accommodation in Edinburgh during the popular Edinburgh Festival will be priced higher than the same accommodation in a different month.

## What Are The Technical Details?

Airbnb hold their approximately 1.5 petabytes of data as Hive-managed tables in Hadoop Distributed File System (HDFS) clusters, hosted on Amazon's Elastic Compute Cloud (EC2) Web service. For querying data, Airbnb used to use Amazon Redshift but they've since switched to Facebook's Presto database. As Presto is open source, this has allowed Airbnb to debug issues early on and share their patches upstream – something they couldn't do with Redshift.

Going forward, Airbnb are hoping to move to real-time processing as opposed to batch processing, which will improve the detection of anomalies in payments and increase sophistication around matching and personalization.

## Any Challenges That Had To Be Overcome?

One big challenge for the Airbnb data science team was keeping up with the company's dramatic growth. Early in 2011, the team consisted of just three data scientists but, as the company was still quite small, the three could still pretty much meet with every individual employee and fulfil their data needs. By the end of the year, Airbnb had 10 international offices and hugely expanded teams, meaning the data team could no longer hope to partner with everyone across the company.

As Newman puts it: "We needed to find a way to democratize our work, broadening from individual interactions, to empowering teams, the company, and even our community." This was achieved through investing in faster and more reliable technologies to cope with the expanding volume of data. They also moved basic data exploration and queries from data scientists to the teams throughout the company, with the help of dashboards and the Airpal query tool; this empowered Airbnb teams and freed up the data scientists from ad hoc requests so they could focus on more impactful work. Educating the teams on how to use these tools has been key to helping them gain insights from the data.

## What Are The Key Learning Points And Takeaways?

Airbnb are a perfect example of a fast-growing company with ever-expanding Big Data needs. The ability to shift and adapt as the company have grown has, I think, been at the heart of their success. This highlights the non-static nature of Big Data and how your data strategy may need to change over time to cope with new demands.

It's also great to see a data science team so well integrated with all parts of the organization (even if they can no longer meet with every employee!). This not only ensures the data scientists have an excellent understanding of the business's goals but also emphasizes the importance of data-based decision making for employees right across the company. After all, it doesn't matter how much data you have if no one acts upon it.

### REFERENCES AND FURTHER READING

Find out more about how Big Data is central to Airbnb's operations at:

http://nerds.airbnb.com/aerosolve/

http://nerds.airbnb.com/architecting-machine-learning-system-risk/

http://nerds.airbnb.com/scaling-data-science/

http://thenewstack.io/airbnbs-airpal-reflects-new-ways-to-query-and-get-answers-from-hive-and-hadoop/

http://www.washingtonpost.com/news/wonkblog/wp/2015/08/27/wifi-hot-tubs-and-big-data-how-airbnb-determines-the-price-of-a-home/

http://qz.com/329735/airbnb-will-soon-be-booking-more-rooms-than-the-worlds-largest-hotel-chains/

# 26
# SPRINT

## Profiling Audiences Using Mobile Network Data

## Background

Sprint are one of the four big US mobile telecoms service providers with more than 57 million subscribers. This gives them access to a huge amount of data on their customers, who increasingly rely on their mobile devices when going about their day-to-day lives.

In 2012, they founded the subsidiary Pinsight Media, with the aim of taking these data sources and using them to segment audiences for targeted, mobile advertising platforms.

## What Problem Is Big Data Helping To Solve?

Lots of us think of advertising as an annoyance or an intrusion. Generally, advertisers have very little idea about who their message is getting through to, and as a result they spend a lot of money passing on a message to people who just aren't interested in, or couldn't possibly afford, whatever is being sold. When this happens (and obviously it happens a lot – most of us probably experience it every single day of our lives) then advertising becomes irrelevant and the effort and expense that the advertiser has put into getting their message to that person has been utterly wasted.

Targeted advertising as it has emerged in the direct-marketing industry and evolved throughout the digital age is the answer. It attempts to segment in as detailed a way as is possible, taking into account demographic, behavioural and locational data. There is a problem here, though, in that a lot of audience segmentation methods rely to a great extent on self-reported data. People can easily set up social media profiles with false information, for reasons of anonymity, and much of the data generated online is cut off from anything that could tie it to a real potential customer.

## How Is Big Data Used In Practice?

Pinsight Media used network-authenticated first-party data to build up more accurate and reliable (and therefore more valuable) profiles of consumer behaviour, which allow them to offer more precisely targeted audiences to advertisers. This means there's less chance of putting an advert they will find boring or irrelevant in front of them, and a higher chance they'll see something they will consider spending money on.

This is similar to the targeted advertising services that are common today, thanks to the likes of Facebook and Google, but with the major difference that they are primarily built around network carrier data.

Jason Delker, chief technology and data officer at Pinsight, tells me: "Mobile operators in general have focused on their core business, which is deploying robust network infrastructure and feature-rich devices. They've not generally been focused on how to monetize the wealth of data they have. They have focused on metrics like network performance, churn reduction, customer care – and these are extremely important ... but there's this whole other business which they haven't really engaged in.

"The mobile services, social networks and even the device manufacturers that mobile operators partner with have leveraged over-the-top applications and created this ecosystem focused around [targeted] advertising that generates hundreds of millions of dollars, and they've done it using data which is essentially inferior to what a mobile operator has access to."

Pinsight Media have developed their own tool, known as a data management platform (DMP), which is used to create targeted advertising profiles using that unique data, which only Sprint have access to. They combine this with bought-in and freely available external datasets to further refine the precision with which advertisers can target their campaigns.

On top of that, they also develop their own applications, such as weather apps, sports apps and a browser for the social media sharing and discussion service Reddit. This allows them to collect more information, which can be tied to a user advertising ID based on a "real" person, as authenticated through Sprint's user data.

## What Were The Results?

In the three years since Pinsight Media were launched, Sprint have gone from having no presence in the mobile advertising market to serving more than six billion advertising impressions every month, making them a major player in the online mobile advertising game.

## What Data Was Used?

The Pinsight service operates using three main types of data: locational, behavioural and demographic.

Locational data, Jason explains, is: "Multi-laterated data – a result of the 55-million-plus mobile devices we have that are travelling all over the country.

"As a result they are talking back and forth with radio towers – so we take the latitudinal and longitudinal coordinates of the tower as well as about 43 other different fields and attempt to use them to decide where a mobile device is at a certain time.

"If a user is travelling and performing multiple actions throughout the day – whether its text messages, phone calls, app usage, emails – [they] can generate thousands of event records per day and as a result we have a lot of location data that we can leverage."

First-party-authenticated behavioural data comes from analysing the packet layer data captured by probes which analyse network traffic and were originally put in to assess and improve network performance. While the content of these packages is often encrypted (using HTTPS services), the platforms where the data is originating from is trackable. "What we were interested in were the publisher-level details, what are the actual services they are using?" says Jason. "And what was the duration? This means we can start to understand that maybe a person is a part of a particular audience. A person might well be a gamer if 20% of their app usage is spent on Clash of the Clans."

Demographic data comes from the billing information supplied by the customer when they take out the account, augmented by third-party, bought-in data from companies such as Experian.

## What Are The Technical Details?

The Pinsight platform ingests around 60 terabytes of new customer data every day. Data is split between two systems – with personally identifiable proprietary information kept on their own secure Hadoop in-house system – while application data and product platforms are run from Amazon Web Service (AWS) cloud servers.

The team use the Datameer analytics platform for its number crunching and have adopted the "data stewardship" philosophy put forward by US Chief Data Scientist D. J. Patil, where a data steward is selected from within every department with responsibility for ensuring analytics is implemented wherever possible. Data stewards are all trained on the Datameer tool. AWS Lambda infrastructure lets them ingest and manipulate large real-time data streams.

## Any Challenges That Had To Be Overcome?

Of course, mobile data is particularly sensitive and private, owing to the details it can reveal about our private lives. To accommodate this, Sprint's service is opt-in only; customers have to specifically give permission for their information to be used to provide them with targeted advertising.

Jason says: "Sprint is the only one of the four large wireless US operators that by default opts everyone out. Instead, we try to convince them – and it's been very easy to do – that if they actually let us leverage that data we will send them things that are more relevant, so ads become less of a nuisance and more of a service.

"Customers are pretty wise to the fact that those types of service help fund and lower the cost of the core mobile operator services."

## What Are The Key Learning Points And Takeaways?

Mobile operators have access to a wealth of uniquely insightful and, importantly, verifiable data that can be used to make advertising more relevant and efficient.

Much of this data is highly personal, and shouldn't be used without a customer's explicit permission. However, anecdotal evidence seems to suggest that more and more of us are happy enough to give this permission, if it means being targeted with more relevant and less intrusive advertising.

Customer data can provide a very valuable additional revenue stream for companies that put resources into leveraging it. This can be used to drive down prices in the core business and pass additional value on to customers.

## REFERENCES AND FURTHER READING

For more information on Sprint's use of data, visit:

http://www.lightreading.com/spit-(service-provider-it)/analytics-big-data/sprint-plays-by-its-own-rules-too/d/d-id/706402

http://www.ibmbigdatahub.com/blog/sprint-leverages-big-data-gain-valuable-business-insights

# 27
# DICKEY'S BARBECUE PIT

## *How Big Data Is Used To Gain Performance Insights Into One Of America's Most Successful Restaurant Chains*

## Background

Barbecue and Big Data may not seem like the most natural flavour combination but one US restaurant chain, Dickey's Barbecue Pit, are bringing them together with great success. The firm, which operate 514 restaurants across the US, have developed a proprietary Big Data system called Smoke Stack.

## What Problem Is Big Data Helping To Solve?

The idea behind Smoke Stack was to get better business insights and increase sales. The intention was to guide or improve all aspects of Dickey's business, including operations, marketing, training, branding and menu development.

Dickey's were already capturing data from various sources, and the aim was to bring that data together in order to maintain a competitive advantage. CIO Laura Rea Dickey – who is the granddaughter-in-law of Travis Dickey, who founded the chain in Texas in 1941 – explains: "Its biggest end user benefit is bringing together all of our different datasets from all of our source data – whether it's our POS [point-of-sale] system in stores directly capturing sales as they happen, or a completely different source such as a customer response programme, where folks are giving us feedback online or in different survey formats." Another problem that Smoke Stack was designed to solve included "information rot", that is too much data without the ability to analyse it in a meaningful, actionable way.

## How Is Big Data Used In Practice?

Smoke Stack crunches data from POS systems, marketing promotions, loyalty programmes, customer surveys and inventory systems to provide near real-time feedback on sales and other key performance indicators.

All of the data is examined every 20 minutes to enable immediate decisions, as well as during a daily morning briefing at corporate HQ, where higher-level strategies can be planned and executed. As Dickey puts it: "We look at where we want to be on a tactical basis. We are expecting sales to be at a certain baseline at a certain store in a certain region, and if we are not where we want to be, it lets us deploy training or operations directly to contact that store and react to the information."

In addition to its strategic value, the near real-time nature of the data means that operational behaviour can be manipulated "on the fly" to respond to supply and demand issues. "For example, if we've seen lower-than-expected sales one lunchtime, and know we have an amount of ribs there, we can put out a text invitation to people in the local area for a ribs special – to both equalize the inventory and catch up on sales."

Big Data has also been integrated into the process the company use to select which items to put on their menu. All candidates for inclusion on the menu are evaluated by users according to five metrics: sales, simplicity of preparation, profitability, quality and brand. If the items meet certain targets in all five criteria, they become permanent fixtures on the menu of that particular restaurant.

Following a successful trial involving 175 users, the company have now rolled out the programme across the entire chain. Feedback from the trial was both positive and negative (the initial rollout was just a "starter pack"), but the general consensus was that, once folks had had a taste of the Smoke Stack system, they wanted more, or they wanted the same thing with a few tweaks. Owing to the success of the project, Dickey's are now moving to a second phase: the Smoke Ring micro-marketing project.

## What Were The Results?

The restaurant business is highly competitive and, for a company to stay ahead, speed is of the essence. "If a region or store is above or below a KPI – whether it is labour or cost of goods – we can deploy resources to course correct, and we are reacting to those numbers every 12 to 24 hours instead of at the end of every business week or, in some cases, using months-old data. To stay profitable, it is just not reasonable to do business that way any more," says Dickey. Thanks to Big Data, Dickey's can better understand what's occurring on the ground and make quick decisions based on that information. For them, this translates into increased savings and revenue.

## What Data Was Used?

Smoke Stack largely makes use of internal data. This comprises a blend of structured data (such as data from POS and inventory systems, and customer data from loyalty programmes) and unstructured data (such as data from customer surveys and marketing promotions).

# What Are The Technical Details?

Dickey's have a team of 11 people working on the Smoke Stack project, including two dedicated analytical staff, an on-site reporting lead and a part-time solution architect who assists with strategic initiatives. There's also a two-person offshore team trained in both analytics and data integration. But the company also work closely with their partner iOLAP, a Big Data and business intelligence service provider, who delivered the data infrastructure behind the operation. Dickey says: "Even though our team is probably a bit larger than the traditional in-house team for a restaurant business, because [data is] where our focus is it requires a partner."

Smoke Stack runs on a Yellowfin business intelligence platform combined with Syncsort's DMX data integration software, hosted on the Amazon Redshift cloud-based platform.

# Any Challenges That Had To Be Overcome?

One challenge for the chain has been end-user adoption. "We have folks in very different, vertically integrated positions within the company," explains Dickey. "Those folks in the corporate office are based in a traditional office setting working around the reality of the business, all the way down to the folks in our stores on the frontline who are running a barbecue pit and interacting with customers. Having a platform that can integrate with all of those different user types is probably our biggest challenge."

The solution came in the form of a dashboard that made it easy for the whole spectrum of end users to access and understand data. "The interface makes it much easier. It's excellent, particularly for people who you might traditionally think of as more 'analogue' than digital. They came to work for us because they wanted to be barbecue artisans, not analysts." The fact that Smoke Stack is so easy to use means it integrates far better into everyday operations, even with less-technical colleagues. At the end of the day, data that is easy to access and understand is far more likely to translate into *action*. Now, more than 560 users are accessing the 200+ reports that Smoke Stack offers.

Another challenge, as is often the case when businesses move into Big Data, has been finding people with the necessary analytical skills. In Dickey's experience, finding the necessary skills is one thing – finding people who are willing to think outside the box in terms of where they may put those skills to use is quite another. "There is a huge skills gap in the market compared to need. For us, part of the challenge is not only finding folks with the right skill sets – it is convincing them that barbecue really is doing Big Data." In this instance, partnering with an external provider really helped supplement the company's in-house talents. "We have been very lucky in choosing the right partner. We have an account contact in our office at least 20 hours a week and we're working very closely with them at all times – it's closed the gap of what would have been a skills shortage for us if we didn't have a partnership like this."

## What Are The Key Learning Points And Takeaways?

This case really highlights the importance of working with a brilliant partner: one that is willing to work closely with you and that really understands what you're trying to achieve. As Dickey puts it: "We've really been fortunate in finding an excellent partner, and being able to pull together technology that's really met our needs – we've made barbecue and Big Data a kind of strange reality."

Another highlight of this case is how users right across the company – from the boardroom to the restaurant floor – have access to data that helps them improve performance. Central to this is a flexible, user-friendly platform. "This flexibility has been key to user adoption and given us valuable insights. Smoke Stack has bridged the gap for us from data that is merely accessible to data that is valuable, timely, manageable and actionable."

## REFERENCES AND FURTHER READING

Find out more about Dickey's experience at:

https://www.dickeys.com/news/2015/05/29/dickeys-barbecue-pit-gains-operational-insight-across-500-stores-with-advanced-big-data-analytics-in-the-cloud

http://blogs.wsj.com/cio/2015/05/28/dickeys-barbecue-looks-to-cloud-for-edge-against-competitors-like-chipotle/

# 28
# CAESARS

*Big Data At The Casino*

## Background

Caesars Entertainment run hotels and casinos around the world, including some of the most famous names in Las Vegas.

They have hit turbulent times recently, with parts of their operations facing bankruptcy and have been hit with a $1.5 million fine over irregularities in their accounts.

During these proceedings, it emerged that the individual asset most highly prized by the company – above even their property portfolio – was their customer database, containing data on 45 million hotel and casino customers around the world.

Caesars (formerly known as Harrah's) built their business model around Big Data and analytics, to allow them to gain an in-depth understanding of their customers and, of course, encourage them to carry on spending money.

## What Problem Is Big Data Helping To Solve?

The US casino industry has been in decline for many years, in terms of money spent at the gaming tables.

This isn't necessarily a problem if you own a large hotel and gambling facility, though – because at the same time the luxury hospitality sector has been booming. Middle classes have emerged among the developing world's populations, hungry for a taste of international travel and Western-style indulgence.

This means casino operators have to look elsewhere to increase their incomes: customers may be losing less money at blackjack, roulette and slot machines but they are spending more on drinks, food and entertainment.

Different visitors come for different things, though – so gaining an overall understanding of each customer's hopes and expectations from their trip to a Caesars resort is essential to providing them with the service they are expecting.

## How Is Big Data Used In Practice?

Gary Loveman introduced Caesars Total Rewards scheme shortly after taking up the post of CEO in 1998.

In 2003, he told *Harvard Business Review*: "We use database marketing and decision-science-based analytical tools to widen the gap between us and casino operators who base their customer incentives more on intuition than evidence."[1]

Over 17 years, Caesars used the programme to build up data on their customers and offer them incentives: free drinks, meals, upgrades on their hotel rooms or limo rides between venues, based on their spending patterns.

Data on customers' behaviour as they move around the facilities and partake in the entertainments and refreshments on offer is analysed in real time by a 200-strong analytics team based at Las Vegas's Flamingo casino.

This means that if a player who is known to have a particularly high lifetime value metric is seen to be having a bad night at the tables representatives can step in and offer them consolation with free refreshments or tickets to a show. Famously, this generosity extended to offering one particularly valuable (and troubled) customer, Terrance Watanabe, an annual air travel allowance of $12,500 by the casino group to visit their venues around the world.

In practice, the strategy involves building an automated, targeted marketing strategy for every individual customer, using data to understand who they are, and then predictive modelling to assess the best way to incentivize them to spend money. High-spending repeat visitors can expect to be greeted personally on their arrival, told that tables have been reserved at their preferred restaurant and presented with complimentary tickets for evening entertainment.

(On occasion, this went too far, with the company stating that they were "backing off" from their policy of greeting customers by name, as some reportedly found this "creepy and Big Brother-ish".)

In 2011, it was announced that Total Rewards were going social: programmes were launched to incentivize players to link their Facebook accounts to their Total Rewards accounts, and additional incentives were offered to persuade customers to "check in" on social services using geolocation features, and post pictures taken at resorts onto networks.

After the success of the Total Rewards programme became apparent, Loveman stated that he could have applied the same analytical approach and gained similarly impressive results within just about any other business in any industry.

## What Were The Results?

In 2013, Joshua Kanter, vice president of Caesars' Total Rewards programme, said that after years of collecting and analysing data, "Big
Data is even more important than a gaming licence."

Since their inception, the company had grown from being able
to trace the journey of 58% of the money spent in their casinos
to 85%.[2]

The widespread adoption of Big Data analytics has widely been credited as the driving force behind Caesars' rise from an "also ran" chain
to the largest casino group in the country, by revenue.

One key finding was that the vast majority of the business's income
(80% of revenue and nearly 100% of profits) did not come from
holidaying super-rich or Hollywood superstars taking a break from
filming. It came from everyday visitors spending an average of $100
to $500 per visit.

## What Data Was Used?

Data on guests' spending habits is monitored from their use of the
Total Rewards cards, which can be used for everything from making travel arrangements to spending at the tables, to food, drink and
entertainments.

Additionally, video data is gathered from the extensive CCTV networks installed throughout each facility, originally to combat fraud.
Now they have the added purpose of monitoring activity levels in different areas as well as foot traffic along transit zones. This is used to
position amenities where people are most likely to want to buy food
and drink, and allows predictive modelling algorithms to suggest the
most profitable locations.

Customer data is also gathered through mobile apps that make processes such as ordering room service or checking in more convenient, while allowing the business to monitor guests' activity more closely and offer incentives to indulge themselves by spending money at nearby outlets.

Caesars also maintain partnership arrangements with credit card companies, other hotel firms, airlines and cruise ship operators, enabling them to amalgamate their customer data with their own and build a more complete picture.

## What Are The Technical Details?

Caesars' Big Data systems are built around the Cloudera commercial distribution of the open-source Hadoop platform. The system is capable of processing more than three million records per hour through the 112 Linux servers located within their analytics headquarters at the Flamingo.[3]

## Any Challenges That Had To Be Overcome?

Loveman – an MIT PhD with a background in analytics, which was very rare in the Las Vegas casino industry in the 1990s, initially put his skillset to use determining the pay-out rates (known as "holds") for slot machines.

Traditionally, much of this had been done by guesswork: declining levels of spending would be met with minor decreases in the hold, based on the gut feeling of casino managers and irrespective of other factors that could be affecting consumer spending.

By setting up slot machines set to hold at different rates – from 5 to 7% – Loveman built up enough data to realize it took the average customer over 40 hours of playing before they would be likely to tell the difference based on monitoring their own success levels: the insight being that hold rates had very little effect on whether a customer would play a machine.

This led to a decision to set the hold at the higher rate across the whole chain, a move which is said to be directly responsible for $300 million extra in profits since it was introduced.[4]

## What Are The Key Learning Points And Takeaways?

Casinos have a much wider range of opportunities for gathering customer data than many other businesses. As well as gambling, they offer food, drink and entertainment. This allows them to gather more detailed and extensive information than many other types of business.

Recognizing the lifetime value of a business's most loyal customers, and rewarding them on that basis, is a strong driver of customer satisfaction and repeat spending.

Regardless of the shape that Caesars Entertainment find themselves in when they emerge from their current difficulties, they will be remembered as a pioneer in the field of data analytics within the entertainment and gaming industries.

### REFERENCES AND FURTHER READING

1. Loveman, G. (2003) Diamonds in the data mine, https://hbr.org/2003/05/diamonds-in-the-data-mine, accessed 5 January 2016.
2. Britt, P. (2013) Big Data Means Big Benefits for Entertainment: Caesars Exec, http://loyalty360.org/resources/article/big-data-means-big-benefits-for-entertainment-caesers-exec, accessed 5 January 2016.
3. Intel Corporation (2015) Doubling down on entertainment marketing with Intel Xeon processors, http://www.intel.com/content/www/us/en/big-data/xeon-entertainment-caesars-case-study.html, accessed 5 January 2016.

4. Jacobs, R. (2014) Turning data into profit at Caesars Palace, http://insideops.com/rljacobs/turning_data_into_profit_at_caesars_palace/, accessed 5 January 2016.

For more information on Big Data at Caesars, see:

http://www.wsj.com/articles/in-caesars-fight-data-on-players-is-real-prize-1426800166

http://2012books.lardbucket.org/books/getting-the-most-out-of-information-systems-v1.3/s15-08-data-asset-in-action-caesars-s.html

# 29
# FITBIT

*Big Data In The Personal Fitness Arena*

## Background

San Francisco-based firm Fitbit are the market leader in the connected fitness wearables market. Their devices act as fitness trackers, allowing users to track various metrics that help them lead a healthier – and more informed – life. The company sold almost 11 million devices in 2014.

## What Problem Is Big Data Helping To Solve?

Fitbit bases their success on the notion that informed people make smarter lifestyle choices. As such, Fitbit's devices encourage people to eat well and exercise more by helping them monitor and improve their habits. The wealth of data being gathered through Fitbit devices not only helps individuals become healthier but also has implications for employers, healthcare professionals and even insurance companies.

## How Is Big Data Used In Practice?

Fitbit track the user's activity, exercise, calorie intake and sleep. Users have access to real-time information about their habits, and the stats are synced (wirelessly and automatically) from the device to the user's smartphone or computer. A dashboard allows users to track their progress (with helpful charts and graphs) and stay motivated.

Aria, Fitbit's Wi-Fi smart scale, tracks user's weight, body mass index (BMI), lean mass and body fat percentage. The scale is able to recognize up to eight individual users (so the whole family can use it) and keep their results separate and private. The stats are synced to the user's home Wi-Fi network and can also be synced with Fitbit's wearable devices. Again, an online dashboard helps the user set goals and track their progress.

Clearly, health data like this is incredibly informative and valuable, beyond even the individual user. Fitbit aggregate data about fitness habits and health stats to share with strategic partners. Personal, individual data can also be shared, with the user's permission. Microsoft's HealthVault service, for instance, allows users to upload and share data from their fitness tracker with health professionals, potentially giving doctors a more complete picture of a patient's overall health and habits than could be gained just through consultations and examinations. And the implications go even further with the recent announcement that insurance company John Hancock are offering a discount to policyholders who wear a Fitbit device. Policyholders can share their Fitbit data in return for rewards linked to their physical activity and diet. This indicates an increasing willingness among individuals to "trade" their private data in return for an improved product/service or financial reward – all of which is great, so long as the transaction is *transparent*, that is the individual is aware of exactly what data they're giving up and why.

Fitbit are also now selling their trackers and special tracking software to employers such as BP America so they can track their employees' health and activity levels (with their permission). Speaking to Forbes, Fitbit CEO James Park said selling Fitbit devices to employers was becoming one of the fastest-growing parts of their business, so we can expect to see more and more companies monitoring the day-to-day fitness of their staff.

## What Were The Results?

Since their formation in 2007, Fitbit have come to dominate the fitness wearables market, having sold almost 21 million devices by March 2015. The company's growth is certainly impressive; they sold 11 million devices in 2014 alone, compared to 4.5 million in 2014. And their analytic monitoring services are clearly well used by Fitbit wearers. The number of registered users on Fitbit's platform is 19 million (out of 21 million devices sold) – indicating that the Fitbit is more than the latest fitness fad: it's a genuinely useful tool helping millions of people become better informed and stay healthy. The company's move into the employer market shows that Fitbit have a canny understanding of the power of health-related data beyond the individual user, and it's likely the employer market will continue to grow at a phenomenal rate for them.

## What Data Was Used?

Fitbit devices gather a range of structured data from users, including steps taken, floors climbed, distance walked/run, calorie intake, calories burned, active minutes a day, sleep patterns, weight and BMI.

## What Are The Technical Details?

Fitbit do not publically share details of their Big Data infrastructure, but when you take a look at their jobs page it does indicate they may be working with SQL database technology, Hadoop, Python and Java.

## Any Challenges That Had To Be Overcome?

One challenge in the health data arena is encouraging medical professionals to work with data that patients generate themselves. There is a fair amount of scepticism around data that hasn't been collected or verified directly by medical professionals. But, as attention shifts to preventing disease and illness, rather than treating them when they arise, this is likely to change.

Of course, no data is more personal than our medical and health data, so extremely secure safeguards have to be put in place to make sure the information only gets to those who are meant to see it. Despite that, cyber thieves routinely target medical records, and reportedly earn more money from stolen health data than by pilfering credit card details. In February 2015, the largest ever healthcare-related data theft took place, when hackers stole records relating to 80 million patients from Anthem, the second-largest US health insurer. Fortunately, they only took identity information such as names and addresses, and details on illnesses and treatments were not exposed. However, there is a fear that it is only a matter of time until a security breach on that scale takes place in which patient records are lost.

Finally, Fitbit face another challenge for the future: stiff competition from the new Apple Watch and others entering the market. Fitbit are in a strong position but they'll need to keep evolving and seeking out new markets if they're to stay ahead.

## What Are The Key Learning Points And Takeaways?

This case highlights how the Internet of Things revolution has the power to touch every area of our lives, including our health. And, while some people may be creeped out by insurance companies or employers monitoring their activities, it's encouraging to see companies offering clear benefits in return for that data. Too often we give up our data without really thinking about it (by signing up to a free Web email service, for instance, or downloading an app). Any company capturing or accessing individuals' data should be very clear regarding what data they are accessing, and how they intend to use it. And it's certainly fair to offer something in return for that data, whether it's a reduced insurance premium or the ability to easily track your weight-loss programme or marathon training using a service like Fitbit. After all the Big Brother-type scare stories surrounding Big Data, it's this sort of transparency that will help foster customer satisfaction and loyalty.

## REFERENCES AND FURTHER READING

Find out more about Fitbit and Big Data at:

http://mobihealthnews.com/43412/fitbit-files-for-ipo-sold-nearly-11-million-fitness-devices-in-2014/

http://www.forbes.com/sites/parmyolson/2014/04/17/the-quantified-other-nest-and-fitbit-chase-a-lucrative-side-business/

http://www.cio.com/article/2911604/health/insurance-company-now-offers-discounts-if-you-let-it-track-your-fitbit.html

http://techcrunch.com/2015/06/29/the-latest-big-data-innovation-is-consumer-empowerment/

https://blog.fitbit.com/

# 30
# RALPH LAUREN

*Big Data In The Fashion Industry*

## Background

The world we live in is becoming increasingly digitally connected. This trend is having an impact on everything, and fashion is no exception. Wearable technology, often referred to simply as "wearables", is expected to become increasingly popular as the Internet of Things (IoT) takes off – a process that is expected to accelerate with the recent launch of the Apple Watch. Among the big names in high-end consumer fashion that have shown they are keen to embrace this new market is Ralph Lauren, which unveiled their connected PoloTech Shirt at the 2014 US Open tennis tournament. The shirt was released on sale to the public in August 2015.

## What Problem Is Big Data Helping To Solve?

With the PoloTech Shirt, Ralph Lauren are aiming to improve fitness, wellness and quality of life for its users – from everyday customers to professional athletes.

## How Is Big Data Used In Practice?

Sensors attached to silver threads inside the shirt pick up the wearer's movement data as well as heart and breathing rates, steps taken and number of calories burned. The accompanying app, available free on iTunes, monitors the data and reacts by creating custom cardio, strength or agility workouts, on the fly, based on those readings.

In case you're wondering: yes, you can wash the PoloTech Shirt, but you have to remove the slightly-larger-than-credit-card-sized Bluetooth transmitter first. The company are currently looking into ways the device can be shrunk – perhaps eventually ending up the size of a button – or incorporated inside the fabric in a way that makes removing it unnecessary.

And although the PoloTech Shirt is firmly in the realm of sportswear – an industry which already is brimming with smart IoT technology such as the Babolat smart racquet and Adidas miCoach smart ball – Ralph Lauren have plans beyond that. The company made their name with ties, so perhaps the Smart Tie is on the drawing board and will be featured across both fashion and tech blogs in the near future? According to David Lauren, the son of founder Ralph, and in charge of global marketing for the company, "A lot will come in the next few months. We are a lifestyle brand, a major fashion luxury brand. I want to be able to gather this [biometric] information in a boardroom or from a baby in a crib. We'll find new needs and we're just at the beginning." Imagine that for a second: a wealth of data is generated in the average board meeting, not just in what is said, but who says it and the manner and tone of voice in which they say it. Biometric readings of meeting participants could deliver useful information about how we perform under pressure in corporate situations.

In the wider fashion world, Big Data is increasingly playing a part in trend forecasting, in which social media data, sales data and reporting from fashion shows and influential publications are aggregated to help designers and retailers work out what are the season's must-have looks.

## What Were The Results?

The PoloTech Shirt is still in its early days but it's clear from the popularity of other wearable devices, like Fitbit, that there's an enormous public appetite for products like this. The ability to track our biometric data and improve our workouts not only helps improve fitness but also helps avoid injury or "overdoing it" during workouts.

## What Data Was Used?

The shirt itself is effectively one big sensor gathering real-time data on direction and movement, plus biometric data like heart rate.

## What Are The Technical Details?

Ralph Lauren worked with Canadian firm OMsignal on the development of the PoloTech Shirt. Data from the shirt is transmitted to the cloud and analysed using algorithms. The app then uses the insights from this analysis to tailor the user's workout accordingly.

## Any Challenges That Had To Be Overcome?

At present, the removable transmitter is perhaps a little larger than ideal. It's definitely noticeable and this may put some users off. However, the company are working towards making it smaller and more discreet.

## What Are The Key Learning Points And Takeaways?

Speaking to the *Wall Street Journal*, Lauren again stressed how the PoloTech Shirt was just the beginning: "We are setting up divisions within Ralph Lauren to focus on developing all kinds of products across all of our brands."[1] So we can expect to see more wearable technology from Ralph Lauren in the future.

Over the last few years, the major players in every industry have had their eyes opened to the possibilities that technology – and, in particular, connected, data-enabled technology – can offer them. No one wants to be left behind in the Big Data and IoT gold rush. Effectively, all businesses are becoming data businesses.

This is exciting not only for the industries concerned but also for those who work (or want to work) in data science. The huge increase in the number and variety of data science jobs being advertised clearly offers opportunities for those whose aim is to work outside of Silicon Valley and the tech industry. And there are rich opportunities on offer for people with skills in data but with passions that lie elsewhere – whether that's in fashion, food and drink or finance.

## REFERENCES AND FURTHER READING

1. Smith, R. (2015) Ralph Lauren to sell wearable-tech shirt timed for US Open, http://www.wsj.com/articles/ralph-laurens-new-wearable-shirt-for-us-open-1439999079, accessed 5 January 2016.

Find out more about Ralph Lauren's PoloTech Shirt at:

http://www.ralphlauren.com/product/index.jsp?productId=69917696

http://investor.ralphlauren.com/phoenix.zhtml?c=65933&p=irol-newsArticle&ID=2080852

http://time.com/3188902/biometric-ralph-lauren-wearable-tech-shirts-us-open-tennis-polo-tech/

# 31
# ZYNGA

*Big Data In The Gaming Industry*

## Background

Big Data is big in gaming. Take Zynga, the company behind FarmVille, Words with Friends and Zynga Poker. Zynga position themselves as makers of "social" games, which are generally played on social media platforms (rather than game consoles like Nintendo, Xbox or PlayStation) and take advantage of the connectivity with other users that those platforms offer. Their games are also built to take advantage of the Big Data those platforms enable them to collect. At their company's peak, as many as two million players were playing their games at any point during the day and every second their servers processed 650 hands of Zynga Poker.

## What Problem Is Big Data Helping To Solve?

Zynga have leveraged data to provide gamers (or bored office workers) with novel, compulsive distractions. And, of course, to make money.

## How Is Big Data Used In Practice?

Zynga's games and the hundreds of others that work on the same principle – for example the hugely popular Candy Crush Saga – use a business model which has become known as "freemium". Players do not have to hand over cash up front to play them, although they often charge small amounts (micro-transactions) for enhancements that will give them an advantage over other players, or make the game more fun. For example, in FarmVille, which simulates running a farm, you can buy extra livestock for your virtual agricultural enterprise. Arrangements are also in place with a range of "partners" ranging from credit card companies to on-demand movie services, allowing players to earn credits to spend in the game by taking up their offers.

This ties into Zynga's second revenue stream: advertising. While playing, you'll periodically see adverts just like while watching TV or reading a magazine. Here, the data that they pull from Facebook is used to offer marketers a precise demographic target for their segmented online campaigns.

Big Data also plays a part in designing the games. Zynga's smartest Big Data insight was to realize the importance of giving their users what they wanted, and, to this end, they monitored and recorded how their games were being played, using the data gained to tweak gameplay according to what was working well. For example, animals, which played mostly a background role in early versions, were made a more prominent part of later games when the data revealed how popular they were with gamers. In short, Zynga use data to understand what gamers like and don't like about their games.

Game developers are more aware than ever of the huge amount of data that can be gained, when every joystick twitch can be analysed to provide feedback on how gamers play games and what they enjoy. Once a game has been released, this feedback can be analysed to find out if, for example, players are getting frustrated at a certain point, and a live update can be deployed to make it slightly easier. The idea is to provide the player with a challenge that remains entertaining without becoming annoying. Their ultimate aim is always to get players gaming for as long as possible – either to feel like they are getting value for money if it was a game they paid for or so that they can be served plenty of ads if it's a free game.

Zynga make their data available to all employees, so they can see what has proved popular in games. So, even a FarmVille product manager can see the Poker data and see how many people have done a particular game action, for example. This transparency helps foster a data-driven culture and encourages data experimentation across the company. Indeed, Yuko Yamazaki, head of analytics at Zynga, tells me that the company are currently running over 1000 experiments on live products at the time of writing, continually testing features and personalizing game behaviours for their players. Zynga's analytics team also do "data hackathons", using their data and use cases, and they host many analytics and data meet-ups on-site. All this helps encourage innovation and strengthen the data-driven culture.

Elsewhere in the gaming industry, it has even been suggested that Microsoft's $2.5 billion acquisition of Minecraft last year was because of the game's integrated data mining capabilities, which Microsoft could use in other products. Minecraft, the extremely popular world-building game, is based around a huge database containing the thousands of individual items and objects that make up each world. By playing the game, the player is essentially manipulating that data to create their desired outcome in the game. Minecraft, in Microsoft's opinion, provides an ideal introduction for children to the principles of structuring and manipulating digital data to build models that relate in some way to the real world.

## What Were The Results?

Zynga measure success on two factors: internal adoption of systems and external player retention. Looking at the internal metric first, Zynga have 2000 employees, all of whom have access to the company's data-visualization tool. At least 1000 employees are using the tool on a daily basis, demonstrating that the company have a really strong culture of data-based decision making. Externally, user numbers are around 20–25 million active daily users, which is a long way from their peak of 72 million active daily users in 2012. A number of factors are at play in this decline, including the end of Zynga's special relationship with Facebook in 2012, and their historical focus on browser-based games (as opposed to mobile-based games). But, in 2014, Zynga acquired mobile specialists NaturalMotion, perhaps signalling a change of focus for the future.

"Compared to Web gaming," Yamazaki explains, "mobile gaming has its own challenges, such as anonymous play activities, more genres of games and more concentrated session activities." Particularly in mobile games, session length can be more important than the number of users, and longer sessions mean greater opportunities for Zynga. This is because in mobile sessions, players are usually paying attention the whole time during their sessions (whereas in a browser-based session, they may just have the page open on an inactive tab). So, though the number of daily active users is down, a stronger focus on mobile games will provide Zynga with the potential for greater reach and higher revenue.

## What Data Was Used?

Zynga capture structured data on everything that happens in their games – almost every single play is tracked, amounting to around 30–50 billion rows of data a day.

## What Are The Technical Details?

At the time of writing, Zynga are in the process of replacing their MemSQL database technology with MySQL SSD, running on Amazon Web Services. Their Vertica Data Warehouse is the world's largest to run on Amazon.

In terms of future developments, the company are exploring real-time analytics and cloud analytics. Zynga have also started investing more in machine learning. And, in addition to the technology mentioned above, they now have a Hadoop/MapReduce environment for advanced machine-learning capabilities, focused on prediction, lookalike, social graph and clustering analytics.

## Any Challenges That Had To Be Overcome?

Zynga's marketing and sometimes intrusive presence on our social media screens has certainly come in for criticism, and it's fair to say the company's fortunes have declined in recent years – partly because of the ending of their close relationship with Facebook and partly because, in the tech world, there is always something new, shiny and often also free popping up to draw users elsewhere. The challenge for Zynga is more where to go from here, although rising mobile user numbers and new game launches offer some bright rays of hope.

## What Are The Key Learning Points And Takeaways?

Zynga serve as a good example of a business built on innovative use of data from the ground up, and heralded the arrival of Big Data as a force for change in the gaming industry. Their culture of data-based decision making is admirable – something a lot of companies can learn from – and will hopefully stand them in good stead for the challenges ahead. As Yamazaki says: "Social gaming continues to evolve – from the way players play games to what features are available on devices … Zynga has killer infrastructure and insane data collection, holding records on billions of installs since its company launch. Big Data has always been Zynga's Secret Sauce to launch it ahead of the competition, and will be a key to Zynga's continued leadership in the space."

## REFERENCES AND FURTHER READING

Find out more about Zynga's journey at:

https://www.zynga.com/blogs/engineering

http://venturebeat.com/2015/07/23/lessons-from-zynga-data-is-essential-but-it-shouldnt-rule-your-world/

http://www.it-director.com/enterprise/technology/content.php?cid= 15336

http://www.forbes.com/sites/greatspeculations/2015/02/18/zynga-posts-disappointing-quarterly-results-and-future-guidance/

# 32
# AUTODESK

## How Big Data Is Transforming The Software Industry

## Background

Autodesk are a Californian software publisher with the core business of developing commercial computer-aided design (CAD) software. Starting with AutoCAD, they have gone on to develop specialized applications targeted at individual fields in design and architecture, such as Revit (construction), Moldflow (production) and Maya (graphics and effects for entertainment media). Their products have become industry standards in many of these fields.

Recently, in line with many other big software producers, Autodesk have made the leap to offering their products via a software-as-a-service (SAAS) model. This means they now have access to a far larger volume and richer variety of data on how their customers use their products.

## What Problem Is Big Data Helping To Solve?

Before the arrival of SAAS, companies which developed software had access to relatively little information about how it was used. Usually the only channels for gathering feedback were customer surveys and feedback forms included in physical product packaging. However, software developers were always aware that only a relatively small section of the user base would ever use these. This would be particularly true if everything were going well: realistically, how often do you bother to contact a business whose services you are happy with simply to congratulate them on a job well done?

Of course, just because the software was working fine and the customer was able to do the job they purchased it for didn't mean improvements couldn't be made. Software applications must constantly evolve to keep up with the competition as well as the growing demands of their user base – and customer feedback provides the most obvious and valuable source of direction.

Charlie Crocker, Business Analytics Program Lead at Autodesk, tells me: "In the old world, being able to understand our customer was relatively difficult. We would understand them on a broad wavelength – perhaps every six months or so we would understand them, when they filled in a survey or we invited them into a focus group or went to visit them in the field.

"We had a couple of tools in the products that could collect error reports and that sort of thing, and for a long time that's what we did – we got very successful at it.

"But in this new world, we need to be able to understand our customers on a daily or hourly basis. We need to understand what the bottlenecks are in their customer experience."

## How Is Big Data Used In Practice?

With the product being hosted in the cloud, Autodesk can closely monitor and track just about every aspect of how their customers interact with their products. It also means updates and fixes can be applied at any time. Autodesk's software developers can accurately gather deep insights into how, when and why their products are being used, meaning focus can be shifted to providing support and enhancements for features that a significant proportion of the user base relies on. Meanwhile, lesser-used functionality can be scaled back or removed, if Autodesk's analytics tell them their users are not getting value from it.

Of course, ultimately the aim is to make sure customers re-subscribe to the services they're paying for, when the time comes for them to make a decision. Data relating to how a subscriber has used the service in the last 90 days before their current subscription expires is seen as being the most relevant and is subjected to the deepest scrutiny.

As Crocker told me: "Understanding the user's behaviour and what drives people to renew their subscription is a big deal. Keeping customers is much easier than constantly having to go out and find new ones."

In order to gain additional user feedback, the company also make early, pre-release builds of many of their popular products available through their Autodesk Labs service. This gives them valuable insights into the sort of features and functionality that their users are interested in seeing included in upcoming services, and new plugins and extensions for existing packages.

## What Were The Results?

The most dramatic result has been the speed at which insights into user behaviour can be gained, and consequently the reduction in time before action can be taken on them. This has led to a distinct closing of the gap between issues being highlighted as problematic by user actions and a solution being deployed. Crocker said: "It used to take six weeks for a signal that started in one of our products to end up in our data lakes. Now with these SDKs it can show up in a couple of hours."

## What Data Was Used?

Autodesk monitor around 600 data points on how each of their users interact with their cloud-based SAAS platforms. The length of time a user is engaging with the service, as well as precise details on what functionality is accessed and what is ignored, are recorded and stored for analysis. They also include internal business data such as transactional records into their equations so the overall expected lifetime value of a customer can be taken into account, and features which attract the big spenders can receive priority attention.

They also monitor how frequently the inbuilt support channels, such as live customer service, online chat and support forums, are accessed, and data from these sources shows where people are having problems and gives clues as to what actions could be taken to pre-emptively solve them.

One indicator that remedial work needs to be concentrated in a particular area is when one issue is generating a higher-than-average number of one-to-one contacts with customer services, via telephone, live chat or email. Data showed that these problems were disproportionately expensive in terms of time spent by Autodesk responding to customer service contact. At one point, one such problem revolved around failed attempts to activate products by entering registration keys. When it became apparent how expensive it was becoming for Autodesk to respond to technical service contacts, further resources were allocated to the development teams working to fix the bugs which were causing the problems.

## What Are The Technical Details?

Autodesk have gathered around 800 terabytes of data on how their customers are interacting with their cloud-based services, and are currently accumulating it at a rate of 100 gigabytes a day. The company use a distributed storage network running Hadoop on Amazon

S3 servers, which they analyse with Amazon Elastic Map Reduce. Other Big Data technologies and platforms used include Datameer, Splunk, Amazon Redshift, Hive and Google's BigQuery engine.

## Any Challenges That Had To Be Overcome?

In the old days, the initial cost of providing a new customer with a service would have been limited to sending them a DVD and instruction manual in the post. While this has been eliminated by the SAAS model, each customer now brings ongoing costs, in terms of computer resources that must be made available for their needs. This means each customer now has an ongoing "running cost". Crocker says: "Every customer has a cost, so we have to understand that or it will be very difficult to provide our services and still make money and keep the shareholders happy.

"As the number of users goes up, we will continue to drive cost consciousness. We're able to now understand which parts of the system are being used most, and which are cost inefficient. You cannot operate without deep visibility into that information, and that information is structured and unstructured – it's messy, but there is amazing context within it."

## What Are The Key Learning Points And Takeaways?

The focus away from a "ship and move on to the next product" mentality towards providing a constantly updated and evolving cloud-based service has brought technical problems and data headaches but has also provided businesses with opportunities to far more deeply understand and connect with their customers.

Capitalizing on this – in order to mitigate the increased cost of providing cloud customers with ongoing processing bandwidth and storage – is the key to success in the era of Big Data-driven SAAS.

By integrating data analytics into customer services and product development, these businesses have the opportunity to more closely match their offerings to what their customers want. Eliminating any middlemen involved in the process, such as retailers, inevitably brings the customer and the service provider more closely together. In theory, and as seems to be occurring in practice, this should mean less disconnect between what a customer wants and what a provider provides.

## REFERENCES AND FURTHER READING
For more insights on the use of big data at Autodesk, see:

http://www.splunk.com/view/splunk-at-autodesk/SP-CAAAFZ2

http://www.datanami.com/2015/01/06/hadoop-behind-autodesks-cloud-ambitions/

# 33
# WALT DISNEY PARKS AND RESORTS

*How Big Data Is Transforming Our Family Holidays*

## Background

Family entertainment company Walt Disney are one of the best-known – and best-loved – companies in the world, and their theme parks and resorts bring in 126 million visitors annually. With the recent launch of the MagicBand, Disney are able to track guests' every move around their Walt Disney World resort in Orlando, Florida – from what rides they go on to what they order for lunch.

## What Problem Is Big Data Helping To Solve?

Data from the MagicBand can help Disney learn more about who their customers are and what they want, allowing the company to anticipate customer needs and improve the theme park experience.

## How Is Big Data Used In Practice?

In early 2014, Disney launched their innovative MagicBand: a colourful wristband that helps guests personalize the entire Walt Disney resort experience. Guests can customize the bands before they leave home at My Disney Experience on Disney's website and, when they arrive at the resort, the bands act as a room key and provide access to the park and FastPass tickets for attractions. The bands can also be linked to card payment details, allowing guests to purchase food and merchandise with a touch of the wrist. Kids get a wristband too, which allows the Disney characters around the resort to automatically greet young visitors with their name.

The wristbands are (at the time of writing) still voluntary, but they've proven popular so far: 10 million bands have been issued since launch. Naturally, this creates a whole lot of data that Disney can mine for insights. Data is collected on who the guests are, where they are in the resort, what rides they go on and what they purchase – potentially giving Disney unprecedented insight into audience profiles and their customers' preferences. The data can also be used to analyse real-time traffic flow around the park, line length on popular rides, demand in the restaurants, etc.

For guests, the band means they can plan and tailor their holiday as much as possible in advance. It also adds to the magic of the experience for kids when all their favourite characters know who they are. (For those concerned that this is a bit creepy, parents have to opt in to allow characters to use personal information from the wristbands.) Cool add-on features enhance the experience even further, like the PhotoPass that links ride photos to specific guests via their wristband – so that goofy photo of you screaming on the rollercoaster can be automatically uploaded to your PhotoPass account without you having to do anything.

In addition, with free Wi-Fi across the Orlando resort, guests are encouraged to use their smartphones to make and alter ride reservations while they're on-site, thus creating even more data for Disney to analyse.

# What Were The Results?

It's not clear whether Disney are already mining the data for insights or simply gathering it for future analysis. Either way, it's obvious this is incredibly valuable data that could help Disney improve decision making and enhance the smooth running of their resorts. Importantly, as several reviews in the press show, the bands are already proving a huge hit with families. With the project getting off to such a strong start, we can expect to see Disney roll the MagicBands out to other resorts around the world in the not-so-distant future.

# What Data Was Used?

The MagicBand tracks every move visitors make around the park. The band is fitted with radio frequency technology that works on both a long range (around 40 feet) and short range basis (e.g. where guests have to "touch in" with the bands, like in their guest room).

# What Are The Technical Details?

Disney's Big Data platform is based on Hadoop, Cassandra and MongoDB.

# Any Challenges That Had To Be Overcome?

This project required a substantial financial investment on Disney's part. For a start, free Wi-Fi had to be installed across the Orlando resort, which, at 40 square miles, was no small feat. In addition, the park's 60,000 staff had to be trained to use the MyMagic+ system, which supports the MagicBand technology. Estimates suggest that the programme cost around $800 million. However, Disney obviously expect the investment to pay off in the form of detailed insights and improved customer experience.

In addition, with this much personal data at stake, data security is always going to be a significant consideration and it's something that Disney take very seriously. Speaking to The New IP in 2015, Juan Gorricho, Disney's senior manager of merchandise business intelligence and analytics acknowledged: "As a company, we have very high standards in terms of how we protect the data, where it is stored, who has access to it. As any corporation, we have a corporate chief information security officer and a whole section of the organization devoted to information security – those are all standard things that any company should have and be looking at because it's just not the data that's important, but the network infrastructure that is being protected … I think we are exceptionally conservative to make sure that we are not damaging that trust with the guest."[1] The company is also careful to allow guests as much control over their data as possible, for example by asking parents to select whether characters can use their children's personal information.

## What Are The Key Learning Points And Takeaways?

This case study shows how the Internet of Things is now touching all aspects of our lives, even our holidays. It's not unreasonable to imagine that, in the future, many of the world's theme parks, resorts and even large hotels will be using this wristband technology to gather information to improve the customer experience. But I believe the emphasis always needs to be on actively *using* that data in a positive way, not just collecting mountains of data for the sake of it. It's still early days for Disney's Big Data project and we've yet to learn exactly how they will use the data, but their emphasis on customer trust and individual control over certain aspects of their data is a good sign.

### REFERENCES AND FURTHER READING

1. Miller Coyne, E. (2015) The Disney take on big data's value, http://www.thenewip.net/document.asp?doc_id=713004&site=thenewip, accessed 5 January 2016.

Find out more about the magical combination of Disney and Big Data at:

https://datafloq.com/read/walt-disneys-magical-approach-to-big-data/472

http://www.huffingtonpost.com/shelly-palmer/data-mining-disney_b_7251792.html

http://www.wired.com/2015/03/disney-magicband

http://aboutdisneyparks.com/news/press-releases/mymagic-reaches-milestone-%E2%80%93-10-million-magicbands

http://www.uscitytraveler.com/10-most-popular-theme-parks-in-the-world

# 34
# EXPERIAN

*Using Big Data To Make Lending Decisions And To Crack Down On Identity Fraud*

## Background

Experian are best known for providing credit references, used by banks and financial services companies to assess risk when deciding whether to lend money.

They also provide a range of other services based around the data they have collected, such as fraud and identity theft protection. More recently, they have added specialized data-analytics-driven services aimed at helping business customers in the automobile trading, healthcare insurance and small business markets.

## What Problem Is Big Data Helping To Solve?

Banks and insurance companies play a game of chance when they lend money or offer cover: they must be confident that their customer can afford to make the repayments, with interest, or that the value of their premiums will cover expenses incurred by paying out on their claims.

On top of that, cyber fraud and identity theft are both growing problems, with more and more financial transactions taking place online, and customers using online banking portals to manage their accounts. Experian's own research has shown that, while five years ago online fraud was mostly a problem for the rich, today all sectors of society are being targeted by increasingly sophisticated hackers and scammers.[1]

## How Is Big Data Used In Practice?

Experian hold around 30 petabytes of data on people all over the world in their credit bureau database, which is currently growing at a rate of 20% annually.

This data is used to build up a detailed picture of consumers and businesses. As well as holding detailed data on individuals such as their credit history, and demographic information such as age, location and income status, Experian group them into one of 67 types and 15 groups using their "socio-demographic clarification" tool Mosaic. These groups include "urban cool", successful city dwellers owning or renting expensive apartments in fashionable city locations; "professional rewards", experienced professionals with successful careers living in financial comfort in rural or semi-rural areas; and "global fusion", young working people in metropolitan terraces with a wide variety of ethnic backgrounds.

This data is used to segment customers for marketing purposes as well as to assess creditworthiness and insurability.

Experian offer their services to financial companies to help prevent fraud by matching incoming transactions against their fraud prediction model, which monitors 282 attributes – such as the value of the transaction, the geographical locations of those involved and their previous behaviour – to offer real-time fraud detection. Should a transaction show a similar profile to previous transactions that were known to be fraudulent, it can be flagged up for manual review or real-time intervention.

They also provide services to 10,000 healthcare organizations in the US alone, including 2900 hospitals, helping them to assess healthcare claims as well as to gain insights into their patients' financial situations and set up affordable payment plans.

Finally, their services aimed at used car buyers draw data from national databases on vehicle trades, insurance companies and government regulatory agencies to provide information such as whether a vehicle has been in a collision or has other issues, for example structural damage or mileage discrepancies on the odometer.

## What Were The Results?

Experian have said that by integrating data analysis across the entirety of their operation, and treating all of their data as a centralized pool rather than as separate, segregated resources, they are enabling more people to buy homes, expand their businesses and manage their finances effectively.

## What Data Was Used?

Experian collect their data on individuals from lenders, which give them details on how much people borrow and whether they make repayments as well as links between addresses that people have moved from and to, and aliases – when people have changed the name by which they are known. They also harvest large amounts of data from public records such as postal address databases, electoral registers, county court registers, birth and death records (to establish if fraud is being committed in the name of a deceased person) and national fraud prevention services such as the UK's CIFAS system.

## What Are The Technical Details?

Experian host their 30-petabyte consumer reference database on a secure, Linux-powered computing cluster built around Hadoop architecture. MapR Hadoop is used for distributed storage, and the server cores also contribute processing power towards the analytics operations – essential for the high-volume, high-velocity data processing required to provide their services in near real time.

Other technologies put to use include Apache Hive and data visualization tool Tableau to provide graphical feedback to analysts.

## Any Challenges That Had To Be Overcome?

Drawing up a profile of the sort of people who were likely to be targeted was seen as key to identifying and preventing fraudsters from carrying out their operations.

In order to do this, Experian overlaid data from their Mosaic sociodemographic profiling tool over the UK National Fraud Database, showing where and when fraudulent attempts had been made to separate people from their hard-earned money.

What immediately became apparent was that, far from identity theft and online fraud being a problem facing the rich, scammers were targeting the far less financially secure at an equally high rate.

This led to a fundamental reassessment of the way fraud prevention initiatives are applied by banks, insurers and other financial institutions. Rather than giving priority to monitoring high-value business transactions, the majority of analytics and scrutiny is now applied to regular, small-value, everyday transactions, which previously may have slipped through the net.

## What Are The Key Learning Points And Takeaways?

Although there is a lot of misunderstanding about the roles of credit agencies – they do not, for example, as many believe, "blacklist" people who they feel are not worthy of credit – they have an important role to play in ensuring that efficient lending and insurance can take place.

The more data available to help them do that, the better (in theory) the situation for us – losing less money to bad debts, or incorrectly calculated insurance risk, inevitably leads to higher premiums and more expensive credit for all of us.

Cybercrime is no longer just a problem facing the rich and well off. Scammers and fraudsters worked out that security systems were generally geared towards detecting large-scale thefts, and a less risky path is to attempt to commit multiple smaller crimes. Security providers are adapting to this, and shifting focus to monitoring smaller transactions.

## REFERENCES AND FURTHER READING
1. Evans, D. (2014) The changing identity of UK fraud victims, http://www.experian.co.uk/blogs/latest-thinking/the-changing-identity-of-uk-fraud-victims/, accessed 5 January 2016.

For more information on Sprint's use of Big Data, see:

http://www.experian.co.uk/assets/consumer-information/white-papers/Harnessing%20the%20power%20of%20Big%20Data.pdf

# 35
# TRANSPORT FOR LONDON

*How Big Data Is Used To Improve And Manage Public Transport In London*

## Background

Transport for London (TfL) oversee a network of buses, trains, taxis, roads, cycle hire bikes, cycle paths, footpaths and even ferries which are used by millions every day. Running these vast networks, so integral to so many people's lives in one of the world's busiest cities, gives TfL access to huge amounts of data – and the company are now embracing Big Data analytics in a big way.

## What Problem Is Big Data Helping To Solve?

As Lauren Sager Weinstein, head of analytics at TfL, points out: "London is growing at a phenomenal rate. The population is currently 8.6 million and is expected to grow to 10 million very quickly. We have to understand how [customers] behave and how to manage their transport needs." With this in mind, TfL have two priorities for collecting and analysing data: planning services and providing information to customers. Sager Weinstein explains: "Passengers want good services and value for money from us, and they want to see us being innovative and progressive in order to meet those needs."

# How Is Big Data Used In Practice?

TfL use Big Data analytics in three main ways: mapping customer journeys, managing unexpected events and providing personalized travel information. Let's look at each area in turn.

The introduction of the Oyster smartcard ticketing system in 2003 has enabled a huge amount of data to be collected about precise journeys that are being taken. Passengers top up the cards with money or purchase a season ticket and then hold them against a touch point to gain access to buses and trains. In 2014, TfL were the first public transport provider to accept contactless payment cards for travel, and now customers have a no-preparation-required alternative to the Oyster card, where they can simply touch and travel with their contactless bankcard. The Oyster and contactless ticketing systems generate 19 million taps each day that can be used for analysis.

This data is anonymized and used for understanding when and where people are travelling. This gives TfL a far more accurate overall picture, and allows more granular analysis at the level of individual journeys than was possible before. As a large proportion of London journeys involve more than one method of transport (e.g. an overland and Underground journey), this level of analysis was not possible in the days when tickets were purchased from different services, with paper tickets, for each individual leg of the journey.

Big Data analysis also helps TfL respond when disruption occurs. When something unexpected happens, for example if TfL's services are affected by a signal failure, the company can measure how many people are delayed so that customers can apply for refunds. When the disruption is particularly severe, TfL can automatically give refunds to affected customers. Customers travelling with a contactless payment card will have their travel automatically credited to their account. And for Oyster customers, TfL predict where a customer will be travelling next, so that the refund is waiting at a station to be loaded on to customers' cards the next time they travel. When there are longer-term planned disruptions, TfL use historical patterns to judge where customers are likely to be headed to and plan alternative services to meet that demand. They can also let their customers know how they'll be affected with personalized updates.

This personalized approach to travel information is another key emphasis for the company. Travel data is also used to identify customers who regularly use specific routes and send tailored travel updates to them. "If we know a customer frequently uses a particular station, we can include information about service changes at that station in their updates. We understand that people receive a lot of email these days so too much can be overwhelming. We focus on sending specific and relevant information to our customers," says Sager Weinstein.

## What Were The Results?

TfL have a clearer picture than ever before of how people are moving around London's transport system, right down to individual journeys. This allows them to understand load profiles (how crowded a particular bus or range of buses are at a certain time), plan interchanges, minimize walk times and plan other services such as TfL's retail offering in stations.

In short, data helps TfL provide a better service to customers. Sager Weinstein cites an example where Wandsworth Council were forced to close Putney Bridge – where buses made 110,000 journeys over the bridge over a week – for emergency repairs. "We were able to work out that half of the journeys started or ended very close to Putney Bridge. The bridge was still open to pedestrians and cyclists, so we knew those people would be able to cross and either reach their destination or continue their journey on the other side. Either they lived locally or their destination was local. The other half were crossing the bridge at the halfway point of their journey. In order to serve their needs we were able to set up a transport interchange and increase bus services on alternate routes. We also sent personalized messages to all those travelling in the area about how their journey was likely to be affected."

The personalized travel emails have proved particularly helpful, with 83% of passengers rating the service as "useful" or "very useful". Not bad when you consider that complaining about the state of public transport is considered a hobby by many British people!

## What Data Was Used?

The company use a range of data collected through ticketing systems, sensors attached to vehicles and traffic signals, surveys and focus groups and, of course, social media. "We use information from the back-office systems for processing contactless payments, as well as Oyster, train location and traffic signal data, cycle hire and the congestion charge," says Sager Weinstein. They also take into account information on special events – such as the Rugby World Cup and cycling events such as when the Tour de France passed through London – so that they can identify and notify people likely to be affected.

## What Are The Technical Details?

TfL's systems run on a variety of legacy transactional platforms as well as state-of the-art technology systems implemented when new assets are delivered. And integrating state-of-the-art data collection strategies with legacy systems is never a piece of cake in a city where the public transport system has operated since 1829. TfL have therefore had to carefully plan out how best to integrate the variety of data sources together. There is always a risk in technology projects that the systems integrations challenges swamp the original underlying business drivers, and projects can quickly become unwieldy to deliver. So TfL took a very practical approach to build their customer data warehouse.

TfL tested the business benefits of their Big Data approach before building new system software and tools. They started with SQL analysis on a small reporting area of the transactional system used for revenue collection. And with the possibility of such exciting and useful analysis, the rest of the company lapped up the analysis and demanded more. TfL then decided to invest in a parallel data warehouse tool that also offers state-of-the-art open-source analytic services as well. The analytic platform effectively gives TfL 150 terabytes of space for a business-analysis reporting suite, as well as a playpen area to test out new data tools and algorithms through "proof of concept" tests (POCs) delivered through the agile software development process. Once these POCs are evaluated, if they provide business benefits, they will be industrialized into the core operationally supported data warehouse. Plans for future development include increasing the capacity for real-time analytics and working on integrating an even wider range of data sources, to better plan services and inform customers.

## Any Challenges That Had To Be Overcome?

On the London Underground (aka the Tube), passengers are used to "touching in and out" – tickets are validated (by automatic barriers) at the start and end of a journey. This is because fares are charged on a zonal basis. However, on buses, there is a flat fare so passengers only need to touch in. There is no mechanism for recording where a passenger leaves the bus because their fare is not based on the distance they have travelled. "This was a challenge to us, in terms of tracking customer journeys," says Sager Weinstein. So TfL worked with MIT, one of the academic institutions with which they have a research partnership, to devise a Big Data solution. "We wanted to know if we could use Big Data to answer previously unknown questions. We had some journey data to show where customers had touched in so we had to start with that and fill in the blanks. We asked, 'Can we use Big Data to infer where someone exited?' We know where the bus is, because we have location data and we have Oyster data for our customers' boardings," says Sager Weinstein. "What we do is look at an anonymized customer's travel record to see where the next touch is. If we see the next touch follows shortly after and is at the entry to a Tube station, we know we are dealing with one multi-modal journey using bus and Tube."

## What Are The Key Learning Points And Takeaways?

Big Data has clearly played a big part in re-energizing London's transport network. But, importantly, it is clear it has been implemented in a smart way, with eyes firmly on the prize. "One of the most important questions is always, 'Why are we asking these questions?'" explains Sager Weinstein. It is important to realize that sometimes the insights we get from Big Data analytics are only "interesting to know". It is important to find a business case. Weinstein said: "We always try to come back to the bigger questions – growth in London and how we can meet that demand – by managing the network and infrastructure as efficiently as possible."

Understanding what you want to achieve is key to using data successfully. It's all too easy to get distracted by the enormous possibilities of Big Data, so it helps to maintain a strong focus on your unique goals and challenges and focus on accessing the data that helps meet them.

### REFERENCES AND FURTHER READING
Find out more about how TfL are using Big Data to enhance the customer experience at:

https://tfl.gov.uk/cdn/static/cms/documents/big-data-customer-experience.pdf

# 36
# THE US GOVERNMENT
*Using Big Data To Run A Country*

## Background

After committing to a $200 million investment in data analytics and pledging to make as much Government-gathered data as possible available to the public, Barack Obama was called "The Big Data president" by *The Washington Post*.[1]

Not all of the Obama administration's work with collecting and analysing data (usually our data...) was well received, of course. Obama's presidency will go down in history as the point when we first began to realize the scale of the covert surveillance being carried out against the domestic population, thanks to Edward Snowden and WikiLeaks.

The administration have made some moves towards transparency, however, such as building the public data.gov portal through which they have promised to make their collected data available to everyone. For better or worse, Obama's presidency has coincided with the huge explosion in data gathering, storing and analysis that we call Big Data – and his administration have been clear they want their slice of the action.

# What Problem Is Big Data Helping To Solve?

Administering the world's leading economic power and its population of 300 million-plus people clearly takes a colossal amount of effort and resources. The federal Government have responsibility for national security, economic security, healthcare, law enforcement, disaster recovery, food production, education and just about every other aspect of their citizens' lives.

These responsibilities have always been divided amongst the many far-reaching arms of the administration – each of which has traditionally collected its own relevant data in the ways it best sees fit, and siloed it away in isolation. Requests to share data between branches of Government would often take time and become mired in bureaucracy and red tape – certainly not an environment conducive to the super-fast analytics and comprehensive data-monitoring techniques which have been revolutionizing private-sector industry.

Earlier this year, the US Government appointed the country's first-ever chief data scientist: D. J. Patil, and before taking it up he had been employed at the Department of Defence, where he analysed social media attempting to detect terrorism threats. He has also held positions at LinkedIn, Skype, PayPal and eBay.

# How Is Big Data Used In Practice?

The US Government have instigated a large number of data-driven strategies among their numerous departments and agencies, each in line with the remit of that particular branch. These include networks of automated licence plate recognition (ALPR) scanners and monitors tracking the flow of car, train and air passengers to discern where infrastructure investment is needed. ALPR is also used by law enforcement to predict and track the movement of criminals around the country, as well as terror suspects. Predictive technologies are also used by law enforcement bodies to anticipate "hot spots", where trouble is likely to flare up and allocate resources according to priority.

In education, because more and more learning at schools and colleges is being carried out online, those bodies responsible for setting education policy can gain greater understanding into how the population learns, and assess the level of education and skills among the population in a specific geographical area, again allowing for a more efficient planning and deployment of resources.

In healthcare, social media analysis is used by the Centres for Disease Control (CDC) to track the spread of epidemics and other public health threats. And the National Institutes of Health launched the Big Data to Knowledge (BD2K) project in 2012 to encourage healthcare innovation through data analytics.

As well as this, the Department of Agriculture carry out research and scientific analysis of farming and food production, based on Big Data gathered in fields and farmyards. Milk production of dairy herds across the States has been improved thanks to work to identify bulls most likely to breed high-yielding cows, through their genetic records.

The CIA were also partly responsible, through investments, for the rise of predictive security specialists Palantir, which use predictive data algorithms to fight international and domestic terrorism and financial fraud (see Chapter 24).

## What Were The Results?

Last year, a group of White House officials appointed to carry out a three-month review into the impact of widespread Big Data technologies and strategies reported: "While Big Data unquestionably increases the potential of government power to accrue unchecked, it also holds within it solutions that can enhance accountability, privacy and the rights of citizens."[2]

After a thorough review of the methodologies, either currently adopted or planned, they concluded: "Big Data tools offer astonishing and powerful opportunities to unlock previously inaccessible insights from new and existing datasets.

"Big Data can fuel developments and discoveries in health care and education, in agriculture and energy use, and in how businesses organize their supply chains and monitor their equipment. Big Data holds the potential to streamline the provision of public services, increase the efficient use of taxpayer dollars at every level of government and substantially strengthen national security."

In 2014, it was reported that a predictive fraud prevention system used by administrators of the Medicare and Medicaid services had prevented $820 million in fraudulent payments being made since its introduction three years earlier.[3]

## What Data Was Used?

The US Government monitor, collect and analyse a vast volume and variety of data, both through their own agencies, such as the Food and Drug Administration, CDC and local, county and law enforcement, and with a wide range of third-party partners.

This includes climate and meteorological data, food production data from agriculture, statistics on crime and security threats from police departments and federal agencies, population movement data from camera networks and demographic research (i.e. the US Census), economic data from public company records and stock market activity, the movement of people and goods in and out of the country through migration and import/export data, patterns of energy distribution and usage, scientific data collected through federal research and development facilities, epidemiology data from tracking the spread of illness and illness-causing bacteria and information related to the effects of climate change through the Climate Data Initiative.

Huge amounts of this data are made available through a set of APIs published on the data.gov website, so they can be shared amongst departments as well as with private-sector innovators and NGOs which can glean insights from them.

## What Are The Technical Details?

Data.gov – the online portal where, by Government decree (the 2009 Open Government Directive), all agencies must make their data available, has grown from 49 datasets at launch to close to 190,000 datasets today. The biggest individual contributors are NASA (31,000 datasets uploaded), the Department of the Interior (31,000) and the Department of Commerce (63,000). The open-source software WordPress and CKAN are used to build and maintain the interface that makes the data available to the public.

## Any Challenges That Had To Be Overcome?

Without doubt, the single biggest challenge facing the US Government in their mission to collect and analyse data has been public trust. The matter is overbearingly political – a challenge which has meant the advantages and disadvantages of any data collection work have to be carefully weighed up, and the impact they will have on the public perception of the administration taken into account.

Since Snowden, there have been widespread calls from both ends of the political spectrum for greater transparency into governmental data collection – which, when carried out without the knowledge of its subjects, is widely perceived simply as "spying". This was undoubtedly the stimulus for Obama's Open Data Initiative as well as ongoing efforts to increase public understanding of the work carried out by Patil and the Office of Science and Technology Policy. The 2014 report to the Executive Office of the President also contains numerous warnings over the danger of the administration becoming seen as too keen to stick their noses into the private lives of citizens, and lists a number of precautions that could be taken to stop this becoming too problematic – chief among them being improved transparency.

## What Are The Key Learning Points And Takeaways?

Big Data holds a great deal of potential for driving efficiencies that could improve the lives of people around the world, so it's critical that governments get to grips with handling it in a way that doesn't generate discomfort or suspicion among their citizens.

Privacy is a huge concern for most people, and it's fair to say that governments in power today have shown themselves to be less than entirely trustworthy when it comes to making distinctions between legitimate data gathering and snooping.

It's clear, however, that many governments in general, and in particular the current US administration, have come to the conclusion that the potential benefit outweighs the potential negative impact of being seen by their electorate as "too nosy". This is evident by the fact that investment in data gathering and analytics is continuing to gather speed, and by the concerted efforts being made by politicians to play down our fears by pointing to increased transparency and accountability.

### REFERENCES AND FURTHER READING
1. Scola, N. (2013) Obama: The "big data" president, https://www. washingtonpost.com/opinions/obama-the-big-data-president/2013/06/ 14/1d71fe2e-d391-11e2-b05f-3ea3f0e7bb5a_story.html, accessed 5 January 2016.

2. Executive Office of the President (2014) Big Data: Seizing opportunities, preserving values, https://www.whitehouse.gov/sites/default/files/docs/big_data_privacy_report_may_1_2014.pdf, accessed 5 January 2016.

3. CMS (2014) CMS cutting-edge technology identifies & prevents $820 million in improper Medicare payments in first three, years, https://www.cms.gov/Newsroom/MediaReleaseDatabase/Press-releases/2015-Press-releases-items/2015-07-14.html, accessed 5 January 2016.

The US Government's open data portal can be found at: http://www.data.gov/

And more information can be found at:

http://www.biometricupdate.com/201308/u-s-government-spending-on-big-data-to-grow-exponentially

# 37
# IBM WATSON

*Teaching Computers To Understand And Learn*

## Background

IBM are the granddaddy of the computing world. Their founding came about through efforts at the turn of the 19th and 20th centuries to use machines to help process US census data. This led to the birth of tabulation-based computing and the dawn of the information technology age.

In the decades since then, IBM have constantly innovated and evolved to keep at the forefront of the industry. Major developments – including the development of mainframes, microprocessors, personal computers and magnetic storage – have shaped the industry into the one we know today. Most recently, IBM have moved to position themselves as a key player in the Big Data and analytics market.

Watson, which first gained fame by winning the US TV gameshow *Jeopardy!* in 2011, is the result of IBM's work to develop what they call "cognitive computing". IBM Watson vice president Steve Gold told me the project heralds the arrival of machines that don't need to be programmed: they can learn for themselves. The Watson system, and the Watson Analytics service it provides, is named after the company's founder, Thomas Watson.

## What Problem Is Big Data Helping To Solve?

Until recently, language has been a big barrier between computers and humans. Computers are incredibly quick at calculations, and their logic is infallible. These are two qualities that make them immensely helpful to humans. However, they can only do what we tell them, and traditionally this has meant giving them coded instructions in a computer programming language. This means that anyone not technically skilled enough to create their own code has to use code written by others, and hope that someone has created a program that does what they want to do.

In addition, computers until now have traditionally only known what we have told them. We give them the information we think they will need in order to solve the problems we think need solving. This introduces elements of human fallibility – we have to know precisely what information they will need, and we have to know precisely what problems need solving.

In theory, computers can "learn" much more quickly than humans. Upload an encyclopaedia onto their servers, and all of the information is ready to be accessed with speed and accuracy far beyond human capabilities. Data analysis has shown itself to be immensely valuable in many fields, from preventing crime to curing cancer, as described elsewhere in this book. But computers aren't, traditionally, capable of teaching themselves anything. We have to work it out first and give them algorithms to follow.

## How Is Big Data Used In Practice?

Connected to the Internet, and accessed through APIs, Watson in theory has the collective dataset of humanity at its disposal. It then uses algorithms developed through a field of study known as machine learning to work out what information it needs, and what it is expected to do. Over time, and given feedback on its performance, it becomes more efficient at this process, increasingly returning more accurate solutions. Watson is constantly updated when valuable information – such as scientific studies – are published, and interactions between Watson and its users are also analysed to help it gain a better idea of what it should be learning, and how it can provide the best answers.

Watson works in a probabilistic manner: ask it a question and it will return a series of likely answers, ranked according to their likelihood of being correct. Many use cases are already being found for this by IBM and over 300 partner organizations already working with Watson. One of these use cases involves improving care for cancer patients. To do this, it reads patient records, studies published in medical journals and pharmaceutical data to suggest the most effective course of treatment for individual patients.

Natural language processing (NLP) is the backbone of Watson. As well as understanding instructions and questions in spoken English, it is learning to understand and help users who interact with it in other languages. This is thanks to partnerships with international businesses including Softbank in Japan and Mubadala in the Middle East. This means a major barrier between humans and computers – the language barrier – is gradually being disassembled.

## What Were The Results?

Watson's first public success was winning the *Jeopardy!* gameshow in 2011, defeating Brad Rutter and Ken Jennings. Its victory proved the success of the system's NLP capabilities, showing it was able to understand the questions, posed in English, to a high enough standard to win the game. It also provided proof of concept for Watson's data analytics and probabilistic modelling technology. Although Watson was challenged with almost every question that the human contestants were asked to solve, one type of question was omitted. These were ones that relied on audio and visual cues. At the time, Watson was not configured to tackle that type of unstructured data.

Since then, it has been put to use across many major industries, including healthcare, marketing, retail, finance, waste management, crime prevention and security. Even toys are becoming more intelligent and useful thanks to Watson – including a robotic dinosaur due to hit the shops in the near future that is capable of giving answers to questions posed by children. As well as being a clever and educational toy, it is thought it may have applications in recognizing the early signs of learning or developmental disorders, such as autism. Another service, developed with Watson by US financial services firm USAA, aims to help leaving military personnel transition to civilian life, by teaching itself about the issues they will face and offering support and advice.

## What Data Was Used?

Watson is plugged into the Internet and can trawl it for information to answer questions or help it learn. In addition, it is specifically kept up to date with particularly valuable information, such as newly published encyclopaedias, scientific studies, news articles and statistics.

## What Are The Technical Details?

Watson's "brain" is made up of 90 IBM Power 750 servers, each containing eight cores, and has a total of 16 terabytes of RAM at its disposal. It uses this to power the IBM DeepQA analytics engines, running on the open-source Apache Hadoop framework. It is said to be able to process 500 gigabytes of information per second.

## Any Challenges That Had To Be Overcome?

Early in its development, IBM's Watson team realized that exposure to a wide range of real-life situations was key to its ability to "learn".

Although IBM are a huge company with employees all around the world, typically they were only ever presented with a limited number of problems to solve – those relating to IBM's business. There was a danger that this could create a bottleneck in Watson's ability to learn and improve itself. To solve this, IBM began to develop partnerships with businesses across a large range of industries, including healthcare, education and finance. This meant Watson was constantly facing fresh challenges and learning to tackle a growing range of problems.

Gold told me: "Our partners have been very creative and very innovative in the ways that they are applying cognitive computing – from veterinary medicine to child's toys, to redefining travel to the in-store retail experience. They are bringing cognitive capabilities to the forefront – working with partner organizations can help accelerate our entry into critical markets."

## What Are The Key Learning Points And Takeaways?

Computers are capable of doing far more than what we tell them to do. Given their speed and accuracy, they can also be extremely good at working out what they should be doing, and are probably far better at spotting problems and coming up with novel solutions than we are.

Without a doubt, we are at the start of the age of the "self taught" computer, and this technology offers extraordinary potential to drive change. The language barrier has always been an obstacle that has prevented us from being able to use digital technology to its fullest potential, but with the arrival of affordable natural language processing we should start to see all kinds of exciting new developments.

### REFERENCES AND FURTHER READING

For an academic paper going into technical details behind how Watson operates visit:
http://www.aaai.org/Magazine/Watson/watson.php

# 38
# GOOGLE

## How Big Data Is At The Heart Of Google's Business Model

## Background

More than any other company, Google are probably responsible for introducing us to the benefits of analysing and interpreting Big Data in our day-to-day lives.

When we carry out a Google search, we are manipulating Big Data. The size of Google's index – its archive of every Web page it can find, which is used to return search results – is estimated to stand at around 100 petabytes (or 100 million gigabytes!) – certainly Big Data, by anyone's standards.[1]

But as we've seen over the past decade, bringing all the information on the Internet together to make it easier for us to find things was only the start of their plan. Google have gone on to launch Web browsers, email, mobile phone operating systems and the world's biggest online advertising network – all firmly grounded in the Big Data technology with which they made themselves a household name.

## What Problem Is Big Data Helping To Solve?

The Internet is a big place – since we moved online en masse in the 1990s, it's been growing at a phenomenal rate and is showing no signs of slowing down. This size itself is a problem: when we have access to practically everything that anyone has ever known, how do we find what we need to help us solve our problems?

Not only is it big, the Internet is very widespread. Information is uploaded to servers that may be located anywhere in the world, meaning anyone wanting to browse through the data available to them is connecting to computers which are sometimes linked thousands of miles apart from each other. Getting individual bits of specific data through to the user doesn't take long, with the speed at which information can travel along copper or fibre-optic cables – a matter of seconds. But that supposes the user knows where the data is located in the first place. Searching the entire Internet even for a very simple piece of information, if you didn't know the precise IP address of the computer on which it was stored would take a very, very long time if you didn't have an index.

With billions of pages of information available online, though, building an index isn't trivial. It would take an army of humans an eternity to come up with anything approaching a comprehensive database of the Internet's contents. So it had to be done automatically – by computers. This raised another problem: how would computers know what was good information and what was pointless noise? By default, computers can't determine this on their own: they have no concept of the difference between useful and useless, unless we teach them and, anyway, what's useless to one person may be critical to another person in order to solve their problems.

## How Is Big Data Used In Practice?

Google didn't invent the concept of a search engine, or a Web index. But very quickly after it was launched in 1997, they established it as the top dog – a title it's gone on to hold for almost 20 years.

The concept which established it as a household name in every corner of the world, while its early competitors such as Alta Vista or Ask Jeeves are barely remembered, is known as Google PageRank. (Google have a fondness for making new names for things by putting two words together, but keeping both words capitalized as if they were still two separate words!)

PageRank was developed by Google founders Larry Page and Sergey Brin before they formed the company, during research at Stanford University. The principle is that the more pages link to a particular page, the higher that particular page's "authority" is – as those linking sites are likely to be citing it in some way. Google created their first search algorithms to assign every page in its index a rank based on how many other sites using similar keywords (and so likely to be on the same topic or subject) linked to it, and in turn how "authoritative" (highly linked-to) those linking pages were themselves. In other words, this is a process which involves turning unstructured data (the contents of Web pages) into the structured data needed to quantify that information, and rank it for usefulness.

Google builds its index of the Web by sending out software robots – often called crawlers or spiders – which gather all of the text and other information, such as pictures or sounds, contained on a website and copy them to Google's own vast archives – its data centres are said to account for 0.01% of all electricity used on the planet!

With the information now all stored in one place, it can be searched far more quickly – rather than trawl all around the world to find documents containing the information searchers are looking for, it's all under one very large roof. Combined with PageRank and later developments such as Knowledge Graph (more on this below), it then does its best to match our query with information we will find useful.

## What Were The Results?

At the time of writing, Google accounted for 89% of all Internet search use. Between them, closest competitors Yahoo, Bing and Baidu accounted for almost all of the remaining 11%, in that order.[2]

## What Data Was Used?

Google uses the data from its Web index to initially match queries with potentially useful results. This is augmented with data from trusted sources and other sites that have been ranked for accuracy by machine-learning algorithms designed to assess the reliability of data.

Finally, Google also mixes in information it knows about the searcher – such as their past search history, and any information they have entered into a Google Plus profile, to provide a personal touch to its results.

## What Are The Technical Details?

Google is said to have around 100 million gigabytes of information in its Web index, covering an estimated 35 trillion Web pages. However, this is thought to account for only 4% of the information online, much of it being locked away on private networks where Google's bots can't see it.

Its servers process 20 petabytes of information every day as it responds to search requests and serves up advertising based on the profiles it builds up of us.

The systems such as search, maps and YouTube that put Google's massive amounts of data at our fingertips are based around their own database and analysis framework called BigTable and BigQuery. More recently, the company have also made these technologies available as cloud-based services to other businesses, in line with competitors such as Amazon and IBM.

## Any Challenges That Had To Be Overcome?

Google and other search engines have traditionally been limited in how helpful they can be to humans by the language barrier between people and machines.

We've developed programming languages based around the concept of codes, which we can enter in an approximation of human language mixed with mathematics, and a computer can translate (through a program called an interpreter) into the fundamental 1s and 0s of binary, logical language – the only thing that computers can truly "understand".

This is all well and good if you're a computer programmer, but Google's aim from the start was to put the world's information at the fingertips of everyone, not just the technically elite. To this end, they have moved on to developing "semantic search" technology – which involves teaching computers to understand the words it is fed not just as individual objects but to examine and interpret the relationship between them.

Google does this by bringing a huge range of other information into consideration when it tries to work out what you want. Starting from 2007, the company introduced Universal Search. This meant that whenever a query was entered, the search algorithms didn't just scour the Web index for keywords related to your search input. It also trawled vast databases of scientific data, historical data, weather data, financial data – and so on – to find references to what it thought you were looking for. In 2012, this evolved into the Knowledge Graph, which allowed it to build a database comprising not just facts but also the relationships between those facts. In 2014, this was augmented by the Knowledge Vault. This took things a step further still, by implementing machine-learning algorithms to establish the reliability of facts. It does this by working out how many resources other than the one presenting a particular piece of data as a "fact" were in agreement. It also examines how authoritative those sites that are "in agreement" are – by seeing how regularly other sites link to it. If lots of people trust it, and link to it, then it's more likely to be trustworthy, particularly if it is linked to by sites which themselves are "high authority", for example academic or governmental domains.

The ultimate aim appears to be to build an interface between computers and humans that acts in the same way as those we have been seeing in science fiction movies, allowing us to ask a question in natural, human language and be presented with exactly the answer we need.

## What Are The Key Learning Points And Takeaways?

Google became undisputed king of search by working out more efficient ways to connect us with the data we needed than their competitors have managed.

They have held onto their title by constantly innovating. They monetized their search engine by working out how to capture the data it collects from us as we browse the Web, building up vast revenues by becoming the biggest sellers of online advertising in the world. Then they used the huge resources they were building up to rapidly expand, identifying growth areas such as mobile and Internet of Things (see Chapter 18, on Nest) in which to also apply their data-driven business model.

In recent years, competitors such as Microsoft's Bing and Yahoo are said to be gaining some ground, although Google is still way out ahead as the world's most popular search engine. But with further investments by Google into new and emerging areas of tech such as driverless cars and home automation, we can expect to see ongoing innovation and probably more surprises.

## REFERENCES AND FURTHER READING

1. Statistic Brain Research Institute (2016) Total number of pages indexed by Google, http://www.statisticbrain.com/total-number-of-pages-indexed-by-google/, accessed 5 January 2016.

2. Statista (2015) Worldwide market share of leading search engines from January 2010 to October 2015, http://www.statista.com/statistics/216573/worldwide-market-share-of-search-engines/, accessed 5 January 2016.

For more about Google, visit:

http://uk.complex.com/pop-culture/2013/02/50-things-you-didnt-know-about-google/lego-server-rack

http://www.amazon.co.uk/In-The-Plex-Google-Thinks/dp/1416596585

# 39
# TERRA SEISMIC
*Using Big Data To Predict Earthquakes*

## Background

Terra Seismic are a Jersey-based company established in 2012 with the aim of improving the early detection of natural disasters caused by seismic activity, such as earthquakes and tsunamis. Their mission is "to reduce the risk and damage of earthquakes". They carry out Big Data analysis of environmental factors and historical data to forecast the likelihood of quakes, and make the data available to the public through their Web portal at www.quakehunters.com.

## What Problem Is Big Data Helping To Solve?

Earthquakes and the associated problems they cause – such as tsunamis, aftershocks and public health emergencies – take a tremendous toll on human life. In 2014, 16,674 people lost their lives to them. The rate of fatalities has increased gradually over time, despite advances in medical science and emergency response, owing to increased population density in areas affected by seismic activity. There is also a huge commercial cost in terms of infrastructure damage and emergency response work. Almost a quarter of a million people were made homeless by the 2011 Tōhoku, Japan earthquake. On average, this financial cost is thought to amount to around \$13 billion per year.

Developing nations are often hardest hit by these calamities, and the cost of emergency response and rebuilding infrastructure puts further strain on economies, leading to a further spread of hardship. Despite huge amounts of research over many years, until recently many geologists and other academics have believed that earthquakes are, largely, impossible to predict.

## How Is Big Data Used In Practice?

Terra Seismic have developed technology that they refer to as "Satellite Big Data" which, they say, can predict earthquakes anywhere in the world with 90% accuracy. To do this, their algorithms monitor live streaming data from satellite images and atmospheric sensors, and analyse this alongside historical data from previous quakes. Atmospheric conditions can reveal telltale patterns of energy release and even unusual cloud formations can give clues to when a quake will occur. When predictive modelling techniques are applied to this amalgamated data, far more accurate predictions can be made.

The predictions made by Terra Seismic are used by insurance companies to accurately assess risks of coverage in areas prone to seismic activity. Hedge funds and traders also use them as part of their analysis of how natural disasters affect financial markets, and multinational companies use them to assess their own exposure to risk. In addition, all of the information on forthcoming quakes is made available to anyone who wants it, for no cost, through the Web portal. Government agencies, charities and disaster relief coordinators can all access and make use of it from there.

## What Were The Results?

Terra Seismic say that since they began testing their technology in 2004 it has predicted 90% of major earthquakes. Most quakes with a magnitude of 6-plus on the Richter scale can be accurately pre-dicted to within one and 30 days. When I spoke to CEO Oleg Elshin, he told me that recent successes had included the prediction of the magnitude 6.4 quake which had hit Indonesia on 3 March 2015. Major earthquakes accurately predicted the previous year include the 8.1 magnitude "megaquake" that hit the Chilean Tarapacá region and the 7.2 quake in Guerrero, Mexico.

## What Data Was Used?

Data from environmental monitoring stations on the ground in key areas of seismic activity, live streaming satellite images and historical seismic activity data are all captured and monitored.

## What Are The Technical Details?

In order to extract insights into the probability of earthquakes strik-ing at particular locations, Terra Seismic have created open-source custom algorithms using Python. These algorithms process large vol-umes of live satellite data every day, from regions where seismic activ-ity is either ongoing, or expected. Data is stored and distributed from Terra Seismic's in-house Apache servers.

## Any Challenges That Had To Be Overcome?

Historically, earthquakes have struck without warning, and aca-demics and experts have put forward the argument that they are essentially impossible to predict.[1] This is largely because of the huge number of factors which are thought to contribute to causing them, and many of these are not properly understood. Although through-out history signs have been documented which could be considered warnings (such as snakes pouring from the ground before the 1975 Haicheng, China earthquake), no scientifically valid method of reli-able prediction had been developed.[2] Terra Seismic's challenge is to show that Big Data analysis can provide the reliable, accurate and repeatable predictions needed to properly implement disaster relief, management and rebuilding.

## What Are The Key Learning Points And Takeaways?

Don't believe anything can't be done until you have tried to do it yourself! Predictive modelling and statistical analysis, backed by large amounts of real-time, unstructured data, are showing us that many things can be accomplished which were previously considered impossible.

Real-time analysis of unstructured data (in this case satellite images) can produce unexpected results. Humans may not recognize that a certain pattern of activity in the data correlates to a particular likelihood of an event taking place. But if there is a correlation then a computer will be able to spot it.

### REFERENCES AND FURTHER READING

1. Alden, A. (2016) Earthquake prediction: Mission impossible, http://geology.about.com/od/eq_prediction/a/aa_EQprediction.htm, accessed 5 January 2016.

2. Shou, Z. (1999) The Haicheng earthquake and its prediction, http://www.earthquakesignals.com/zhonghao296/A010720.html, accessed 5 January 2016.

Here is the site where the data and predictions about earthquakes is made available:

http://quakehunters.com/

# 40
# APPLE

## How Big Data Is At The Centre Of Their Business

## Background

Technology giant Apple are officially the world's most valuable brand. Known for their iconic product design and user-friendly interfaces, Apple are in fact more than twice as valuable as the world's second most valuable brand, Microsoft. But, until relatively recently, Apple weren't considered much of a Big Data company. Let's look at how that changed and why.

## What Problem Is Big Data Helping To Solve?

In some ways, despite being the most profitable tech company in the world, Apple found themselves having to play catch-up with Big Data. While Apple traditionally employed teams of highly paid experts in aesthetics and design to produce systems they thought people would want to use, competitors like Google examined user data to see how people actually were using them. This gave those competitors an edge with the everyday apps that made smartphones so popular – maps, navigation, voice recognition and other aspects of computing that we want to do on the move. To cement their position as the leader of the pack, Apple needed to get to grips with customer data.

# How Is Big Data Used In Practice?

It's fair to say Apple have now entered the Big Data race with a strong stride. Their powerful presence in the mobile market has put their devices in the hands of millions and they have been keen to encourage development of apps that are based on monitoring and sharing of user data. A notable example is their recently announced partnership with IBM to facilitate the development of health-related mobile apps. The partnership will allow iPhone and Apple Watch users to share data with IBM's Watson Health cloud-based healthcare analytics service, potentially bringing the benefits of crowdsourced, Big Data-driven healthcare to millions (see Chapter 37). The groundbreaking deal could also lead to further advances in healthcare as IBM's Big Data-crunching engines gain access to real-time activity and biometric data from potentially millions of people who use Apple's devices around the world.

Apple have also provided a range of applications targeted at other industries, including air travel, education, banking and insurance, also developed in partnership with IBM and aimed at bringing analytical capabilities to users of their mobile devices in those fields. The launch of the Apple Watch in April 2015 could accelerate this process in a dramatic fashion – almost three million units have been sold since it launched, helping to bring smartwatches into the mainstream. Designed to be worn all day long, and to collect a wider variety of data thanks to additional sensors, the Apple Watch means even more personal data is available for analysis.

As well as positioning itself as an "enabler" of Big Data in other people's lives, it has also been put to use in its own internal systems. Apple have often been secretive about the processes behind their traditionally greatest strength – product design. However, it is known that Big Data also plays a part here. Data is collected about how, when and where the company's products – smartphones, tablets, computers and now watches – are used, to determine what new features should be added, or how the way they are operated could be tweaked to provide the most comfortable and logical user experience.

The Siri voice recognition features of iDevices have proved popular with users too, and this is also powered by Big Data. Voice data captured by the machine is uploaded to its cloud analytics platforms, which compare them alongside millions of other user-entered commands to help it become better at recognizing speech patterns (an example of machine learning) and more accurately match users to the data they are seeking. Apple keep this data for two years – disassociated from your real identity and assigned with a unique anonymous indicator, as a concession to ensuring privacy.

Like their biggest competitors, Apple also offer cloud-based storage, computing and productivity solutions, for both consumer and business use. In March 2015, Apple purchased FoundationDB, a popular proprietary database architecture widely used for Big Data applications. It is thought this could be used to bring increased analytical prowess across their suite of online services, such as iCloud, Apple Productivity Works (formerly iWork) and their recently launched music-streaming service.

Aiming to capture a share of the market dominated by Pandora, Spotify and Google Music, the new Apple Music service was built on the technology acquired by their 2014 purchase of Beats Music. Beats developed algorithms designed to match users with music they were likely to enjoy listening to, in a similar way to recommendation engines used by Amazon and Netflix. Sales through Apple's iTunes service have declined as the popularity of streaming services has overtaken downloading as the favourite method of accessing music online. The new service, launched in June 2015, is Apple's attempt to get a slice of this action.

## What Were The Results?

While there's no doubt that Apple had a strong track record of understanding what their users wanted, even before the Big Data phenomenon, the company are clearly focused on using Big Data to improve their products and services. Early signs for the Apple Watch and Apple Music are promising; three million Apple Watches were sold in the first few months following its launch, and 11 million iPhone users signed up to the free trial of Apple Music in the space of just four weeks (the free trial converts to a monthly subscription of $9.99 unless the users opt out of the service).

## What Data Was Used?

Apple's focus is on internal data, generated by users of their products and services. For example, the Apple Watch includes sensors such as a heart rate sensor and accelerometer to track user's activities and overall health.

## What Are The Technical Details?

Apple are more secretive than many big companies when it comes to their Big Data infrastructure. What we do know is that Apple uses Teradata equipment to store the masses of data Apple users generate; reportedly, Apple were Teradata's fastest customer to reach petabyte scale.

## Any Challenges That Had To Be Overcome?

Apple didn't provide a comment for this case study but it strikes me that one obvious challenge to overcome is the sheer scale of data that Apple are now working with. Even without recent launches like the Apple Watch and Apple Music, Apple users generate staggering amounts of data every day (just think of the data that Siri alone generates). So, the ability to store all this data is crucial and, as such, Apple are making huge investments in new and expanded data centres; the company announced in early 2015 that they would be doubling the size of their Reno site, as well as expanding their Prineville, Oregon operations. Apple have also announced new data centre projects in Athenry, Ireland and Viborg, Denmark, both expected to be up and running in 2017. These are costly projects, so it's no surprise that Apple are thinking seriously long term about their future in Big Data.

## What Are The Key Learning Points And Takeaways?

Apple may have been slower in their uptake of Big Data and analytics than many of their rivals, but they have clearly seen that they have to play a big part in their future if they want to stay ahead of the pack. It seems likely that Apple will try to use Big Data to move away from hugely expensive, episodic product releases to drive their growth as a business towards the more organic, constantly regenerating model of growth favoured by their competitors in the software and services markets. If Apple can meld their trademark excellence in design and user-friendliness with innovative uses of Big Data analytics, they should continue to surprise us with products and services that become culturally ingrained in everyday life, just like the iMac, iPod and iPhone – ensuring they remain the world's most valuable brand for some time to come.

To me, this case highlights how it's never too late to start working with Big Data in your company. Even if you think your competitors are way ahead of you in terms of generating and analysing data, there's always scope to catch up. Big Data innovation is constantly evolving, so it can be a struggle for any company to keep up with the latest developments, regardless of their size ... but remember the same is true for your competitors, so they may not be as far ahead as you think.

## REFERENCES AND FURTHER READING

Read more about Apple and Big Data at:

http://www.forbes.com/sites/netapp/2012/10/03/google-apple-maps-big-data-cloud/

http://appleinsider.com/articles/15/06/19/apple-ibm-to-take-partnership-into-education-with-predictive-modeling-app

https://www.linkedin.com/pulse/apple-ibm-team-up-new-big-data-health-platform-bernard-marr

http://www.forbes.com/sites/kurtbadenhausen/2015/05/13/apple-and-microsoft-head-the-worlds-most-valuable-brands-2015/

https://datafloq.com/read/apple-re-invent-big-data/452

http://appleinsider.com/articles/15/10/02/apple-inc-massively-expanding-its-icloud-data-centers-in-nevada-oregon

# 41
# TWITTER

## How Twitter And IBM Deliver Customer Insights From Big Data

## Background

Twitter is the world's second-most-popular social network after runaway market leader Facebook, with 310 million users active each month. Since its launch as a "micro-blogging" site in 2006, it has also become very popular with businesses that have products and services to promote.

The San Francisco company employ nearly 4000 people and generated revenue of $436 million in the first quarter of 2015, but have never turned a profit – almost all of their users get the service for free, and the computer power and infrastructure needed to handle that many users doesn't come cheap!

Last year, they announced that IBM would become their first partner in the Twitter Partnership Program, offering other businesses the chance to work with both Twitter and IBM to gain value from data and analytics.

## What Problem Is Big Data Helping To Solve?

Twitter's management know full well that their network needs to take a bigger share than the 0.84% it currently holds of the global online advertising market if the company want to become profitable. Around 88% of their revenues come from promoted tweets, which are messages companies pay to have appear in the Twitter feeds of users who are likely to be interested.

This has to pay the salaries of their thousands of staff, as well as the upkeep and maintenance of the huge computer network needed to keep the service running at no cost to the end user.

Twitter know they need to find other ways of monetizing the content their users create if they want to continue to grow and improve their infrastructure. Part of their strategy for doing this involves offering the vast amount of data that they generate every second of the day to partners with advanced analytics capabilities, such as IBM. They can then sell their analytics services to other, smaller businesses, which can gain their own value from it.

There is a tremendous amount of value in the data broadcast across Twitter, most of which, in comparison to that shared on rival social network Facebook, is made public by those who share it, and so is available for anyone to analyse.

It can give insights into how people are connected to each other, where they stand on political issues, what they buy, where they eat out and just about any other aspects of their lives – a goldmine of information to marketers.

The problem is that the average business does not have the analytics capabilities to capitalize on to the best effect. Anyone can access Twitter and see what people are talking about, but transforming that into valuable, actionable insights is tricky unless you have a firm grasp of the technical details of data collection and storage, statistical programming, predictive modelling and programming algorithms. Essentially, the value stored in social media goes to waste when companies do not have the skills or infrastructure to capitalize on it.

## How Is Big Data Used In Practice?

In a nutshell, IBM create value from the data that Twitter collect as their users tweet – all of the 6000 tweets that are posted every second are available for IBM to analyse in real time through their "firehose" API.

Other businesses can then access Twitter's data through IBM's tools, which they can use to derive their own data-driven insights.

Thousands of specialist staff are said to have been trained by IBM and Twitter to work with businesses on a consultancy basis, to help them translate the Twitter data into actions.

As of the time of writing, the service has only just been made openly available. However, in the first half of 2015, Twitter partnered with various businesses to trial the technology. These partners included a communications company that aimed to reduce customer churn rate by working out where their service was likely to be affected by bad weather by monitoring social media chatter, and distributing resources to reduce service downtime.

Another use case involved a food and drink retailer which was able to deduce that the spending patterns of their most loyal customers were affected by staff turnover in retail outlets – establishing a firm link between high staff turnover and low customer loyalty. In other words, recognizable, regular faces behind the counter encouraged high-spending customers to return more frequently.

## What Were The Results?

The programme has only just kicked off, at the time of writing, and so not much data is available on real-world results. However, Twitter say that the unnamed telecommunications company they partnered with during the trial phase were able to reduce customer churn by 5% by using their data in combination with the tools provided by IBM.

## What Are The Technical Details?

Twitter are a huge data resource. Their 310 million monthly active users post 500 million messages a day, with each of those messages potentially offering valuable insights into real lives.

Twitter and IBM make their analytical tools available through three services: IBM Big Insights for Twitter, Watson Analytics with Twitter (which uses the advanced Watson cognitive computing system I talk about in Chapter 37) and as part of their BigInsights Enterprise Hadoop service.

## Any Challenges That Had To Be Overcome?

So far, the service only seems to involve textual analysis of written content posted to Twitter. Increasingly, consumers are interacting with social media through pictures and videos, which offer a whole new set of challenges to Big Data miners looking for insights.

Image-led social media services such as Instagram are still lagging behind Facebook and Twitter, but are catching up in terms of the amount of unstructured data (photos and videos) uploaded every day. Other services have already begun mining this data for information. One service, for example, allows brands to recognize when pictures of their products are uploaded, and judge the mood of the people shown in the pictures with the products using facial-recognition systems. Later changes to Twitter mean huge amounts of visual data are now uploaded to the network, along with the 140-word text messages that are the company's bread and butter, but no case studies have been made available of this data being analysed through the IBM and Watson partnership.

# What Are The Key Learning Points And Takeaways?

Social media is a rich source of insights into consumer sentiment and behaviour.

Much of that data is locked away because of its sheer quantity, which makes drawing meaningful insights difficult – the noise-to-signal ratio is weighted towards noise owing to the sheer amount of background chatter.

Establishing partnerships enables companies that are data-rich, such as social media networks, to work with companies that have advanced analytic capabilities. Between them, they can create something more valuable than either of them could manage alone.

## REFERENCES AND FURTHER READING

For more information on Twitter and social media analytics, see:

http://expandedramblings.com/index.php/march-2013-by-the-numbers-a-few-amazing-twitter-stats

http://www.amazon.com/Mining-Social-Web-Facebook-LinkedIn-ebook/dp/B00FNBWNLU/ref=sr_1_2?ie=UTF8&qid=1440609232&sr=8-2&keywords=twitter+analytics

http://fortune.com/2014/11/03/ibm-twitter-data-analytics/

http://www.ibm.com/big-data/us/en/big-data-and-analytics/ibmandtwitter.html

# 42
# UBER

*How Big Data Is At The Centre Of Uber's Transportation Business*

## Background

Uber is a smartphone app-based taxi booking service which connects users who need to get somewhere with drivers willing to give them a ride. The service has been hugely popular. Since being launched to serve San Francisco in 2009, the service has been expanded to many major cities on every continent except for Antarctica, and the company are now valued at $41 billion. The business are rooted firmly in Big Data, and leveraging this data in a more effective way than traditional taxi firms has played a huge part in their success.

## What Problem Is Big Data Helping To Solve?

Uber's entire business model is based on the very Big Data principle of crowdsourcing: anyone with a car who is willing to help someone get to where they want to go can offer to help get them there. This gives greater choice for those who live in areas where there is little public transport, and helps to cut the number of cars on our busy streets by pooling journeys.

## How Is Big Data Used In Practice?

Uber store and monitor data on every journey their users take, and use it to determine demand, allocate resources and set fares. The company also carry out in-depth analysis of public transport networks in the cities they serve, so they can focus coverage in poorly served areas and provide links to buses and trains.

Uber hold a vast database of drivers in all of the cities they cover, so when a passenger asks for a ride, they can instantly match you with the most suitable drivers. The company have developed algorithms to monitor traffic conditions and journey times in real time, meaning prices can be adjusted as demand for rides changes, and traffic conditions mean journeys are likely to take longer. This encourages more drivers to get behind the wheel when they are needed – and stay at home when demand is low. The company have applied for a patent on this method of Big Data-informed pricing, which they call "surge pricing". This is an implementation of "dynamic pricing" – similar to that used by hotel chains and airlines to adjust price to meet demand – although rather than simply increasing prices at weekends or during public holidays it uses predictive modelling to estimate demand in real time.

Data also drives (pardon the pun) the company's UberPool service, which allows users to find others near to them who, according to Uber's data, often make similar journeys at similar times so that they can share a ride. According to Uber's blog, introducing this service became a no-brainer when their data told them the "vast majority of [Uber trips in New York] have a look-a-like trip – a trip that starts near, ends near and is happening around the same time as another trip". Other initiatives either trialled or due to launch in the future include UberChopper, offering helicopter rides to the wealthy, Uber-Fresh for grocery deliveries and Uber Rush, a package courier service.

Uber rely on a detailed rating system – users can rate drivers, and vice versa – to build up trust and allow both parties to make informed decisions about who they want to share a car with. Drivers in particular have to be very conscious of keeping their standards high, as falling below a certain threshold could result in their not being offered any more work. They have another metric to worry about, too: their "acceptance rate". This is the number of jobs they accept versus those they decline. Drivers apparently have been told they should aim to keep this above 80%, in order to provide a consistently available service to passengers.

## What Were The Results?

Data is at the very heart of everything Uber do, meaning this case is less about short-term results and more about long-term development of a data-driven business model. But it's fair to say that without their clever use of data the company wouldn't have grown into the phenomenon they are.

There is a bigger-picture benefit to all this data that goes way beyond changing the way we book taxis or get ourselves to the office each day. Uber CEO Travis Kalanick has claimed that the service will also cut the number of private, owner-operated automobiles on the roads of the world's most congested cities. For instance, he hopes UberPool alone could help cut traffic on the streets of London by a third. Services like Uber could revolutionize the way we travel around our crowded cities. There are certainly environmental as well as economic reasons why this would be a good thing.

## What Data Was Used?

The company use a mixture of internal and external data. For example, Uber calculate fares automatically using GPS, traffic data and the company's own algorithms, which make adjustments based on the time the journey is likely to take. The company also analyse external data such as public transport routes to plan services.

## What Are The Technical Details?

It has proven tricky to get any great detail on Uber's big data infrastructure, but it appears all their data is collected into a Hadoop data lake and they use Apache Spark and Hadoop to process the data.

## Any Challenges That Had To Be Overcome?

The company's algorithm-based approach to surge pricing has occasionally caused problems at busy times – a Forbes article noted how one five-mile journey on New Year's Eve 2014 that would normally cost an average of less than $20 ended up costing $122.[1] This was because of the number of drivers on the road and the extra time taken to complete the journey. Plenty of people would argue that's simple economics: it's normal to pay more for a product or service in times of peak demand (as anyone going away in the school holidays will confirm). But it hasn't stopped the company coming under fire for their pricing policy.

There have been other controversies – most notably regular taxi drivers claiming it is destroying their livelihoods, and concerns over the lack of regulation of the company's drivers. Uber's response to protests by taxi drivers has been to attempt to co-opt them, by adding a new category to their fleet. Their UberTaxi service means you can be picked up by a licensed taxi driver in a registered private hire vehicle.

It's fair to say there are still some legal hurdles to overcome: the service is currently banned in a handful of jurisdictions, including Brussels and parts of India, and is receiving intense scrutiny in many other parts of the world. There have been several court cases in the US regarding the company's compliance with regulatory procedures – some of which have been dismissed and some are still ongoing. But, given their popularity, there's a huge financial incentive for the company to press ahead with their plans to transform private travel.

# What Are The Key Learning Points And Takeaways?

Uber demonstrate how even your very business model can be based on Big Data – with outstanding results. And Uber are not alone in this realization. They have competitors offering similar services on a (so far) smaller scale such as Lyft, Sidecar and Haxi. Providing the regulation issues can be overcome, competition among these upstarts is likely to be very fierce. The most successful company is likely to be the one that manages to best use the data available to them to improve the service they provide to customers.

## REFERENCES AND FURTHER READING

1. Worstall, T. (2015) So Uber and Lyft's surge pricing worked just perfectly on New Year's Eve then, http://www.forbes.com/sites/timworstall/2015/01/03/so-uber-and-lyfts-surge-pricing-worked-just-perfectly-on-new-years-eve-then/, accessed 5 January 2016.

Read more about Uber's plans to revolutionize the way we move around our cities at:

http://newsroom.uber.com/

http://newsroom.uber.com/la/2015/02/uber-and-las-public-transportation-working-together/

http://www.cityam.com/1412567312/uber-s-plan-rid-city-million-cars

# 43
# ELECTRONIC ARTS

*Big Data In Video Gaming*

## Background

Electronic Arts (EA) are one of the world's biggest publishers of video games. They were founded by Trip Hawins, who left his job as director of product marketing at Apple after witnessing the phenomenal speed with which video gaming grew as a pastime in the early 1980s.

Since then the industry has grown and grown, and is today said to bring in revenues of over $100 billion globally.

Because modern video games – whether played on games consoles, mobile phones or computers – are continuously online when they are being played, they are capable of monitoring the behaviour of players in great depth. Every decision or strategy which is played out can be recorded and analysed, to give the game developers insights into what players enjoy, how they adapt to challenges and what is just too difficult to be fun.

In 2012, EA were facing difficulties. Gamers seemed to be spending less on their core products – the shoot 'em ups, sports simulations and epic fantasy games they had scored successive hits with over three decades. On top of that, several widespread changes in industry models – such as distribution and payment, with the advent of "freemium" games – were disrupting their business. Chief technical officer Rajat Taneja unveiled ambitious plans to win back the fans they were losing – by working out how to use all the data they were gathering during online games to give them exactly what they wanted.

## What Problem Is Big Data Helping To Solve?

The world of gaming is extremely competitive – and not just for the players who spend their spare time racing virtual rally cars or shooting each other with virtual guns. Developers and publishers are also having to constantly innovate in order to outdo their competitors. Gamers demand bigger and better games to take advantage of the more powerful hardware available to them, and as a result the cost of videogame production climbs ever higher with each passing year. To illustrate this, in 1994 Origin, a subsidiary of EA, released Wing Commander 3, which had a development budget of $5 million – unheard of at the time for a computer game. In 2013, Grand Theft Auto 5 is said to have cost $100 million. And in 2014, Activision Blizzard said they would spend around half a billion in the coming years on their Destiny franchise. Large-scale, blockbuster "AAA" games typically take at least two years of full-time work by teams of hundreds of people to create and bring to market. But while risks are high, the potential for reward is there to match them. Score a hit and you can sell millions of a product that cost virtually nothing to store or ship, thanks to the adoption of digital distribution across the industry, and retails for $60–$100 per unit.

## How Is Big Data Used In Practice?

Gone are the days when playing a video game was a solitary experience where the gamer was disconnected from the rest of the world and interacted only with the machine in front of them. Most modern video games, whether they are played on games consoles, mobile phones or PCs, have online functionality these days. It's all but a requirement for AAA titles. This serves dual purposes. Not only can gamers race, fight and shoot it out against other players anywhere in the world, the companies running the servers those games operate on can see exactly what they are doing and how their users are interacting with their products. Everything the player does, from buying the game through a publisher's digital store, to chatting with their friends using the social features, to playing the game itself, leaves a rich data trail.

If the number of players losing all of their virtual lives and giving up in frustration at a particular challenge reaches a certain point, analysis can show where adjustments could be made that may lead to a more engaging, and longer-lasting, experience. If the game notices that players who engage with other players over voice chat tend to play for longer, it can examine what features of the game encourage users to communicate, and ensure it is more liberal with their distribution. Keeping players hooked is the name of the game, after all; otherwise, they will probably defect to competitors' products pretty quickly.

These adjustments can be either global – rolled out to the whole user base through software updates – or more personal. By assigning players a unique identifier that can be tracked across whatever platforms they play on, a model of that user's preferences and playing styles can be built up.

As Taneja announced in his keynote speech at the Strata 2013 conference: "Gaming is now being consumed in an always on, always connected, multi device social manner. That changes everything. We are now able to collect so much insight on the game, the gameplay and the gamer that we have to rethink all our fundamental assumptions of the past."[1]

As well as improving gameplay experiences, Big Data is put to use in marketing as well. Most of the big game publishers now offer their own online distribution networks, where games can be sold directly to the player and downloaded right into their living room (or wherever they happen to be if they are playing on mobile). Here, EA, in line with other big players, have built complex recommendation analytics into their Origin service, which matches the player with games and promotions most likely to appeal, based on the information that the system has about them, and others who fit their profile. Many games today also feature micro-transactions – where players can spend a small amount of real-world cash to gain virtual-world benefits. This brings added revenue for the publishers to help meet those development costs, and hopefully provides the shareholders with a little bonus too.

## What Were The Results?

Between 2012 and 2013, EA took a fall in revenue of 7% – their income fell from $4 billion to $3.6 billion. By the end of 2014, it had shot up again by 22%, reaching $4.4 billion – the company's highest turnover in their 30-year history.[2] Much of this was attributed to the efforts that had been put into reconnecting with disaffected customers – which was possible thanks to concentrated efforts to use their data to understand them.

## What Data Was Used?

EA collect data such as names and geographical information from players when they sign up to their services. They then track their use of the Origin game portal to learn what games they like to browse and eventually buy.

Once the game is installed on a user's machine, be that a console, phone or PC, it can gather information about that device. If their user connects their social media account (to make it easier to find and play games with their friends), it can learn everything they share on there.

In game, every motion and action the player puts into the game controller or touchscreen interface can be tracked to build a profile of how they like to play. This allows them to determine whether they are a cautious player or more gung-ho in their approach to overcoming problems.

## What Are The Technical Details?

EA host 50 billion minutes of online gameplay in a typical month, consisting of 2.5 billion sessions.

In 2013, it was reported that just one game, Battlefield, generated 1 terabyte of user telemetry data every day. Across all of the games on their network, this figure was roughly 50 terabytes.

EA's Big Data analytical framework is built on open-source technologies, including Apache Hadoop and Spark.

## Any Challenges That Had To Be Overcome?

Like many companies tackling Big Data for the first time, EA soon realized that one of their first problems was that the data was too big, and their existing data systems were not cut out to measure the complicated and messy data their games were collecting from players.

The solution, Taneja says, was: "to take just a small fraction of that data, store it very smartly and then run it through the pipe so that action could be taken in the game, around the game or in marketing after the game".

In order to do this the company rebuilt their data pipeline from scratch, implementing Hadoop to run the machine-learning and adaptive, predictive algorithms they had created to analyse the data.

The final step, Taneja explained, was implementing a unified customer ID to tie together a user's profile across all of the platforms they could be running their games on.

"The secret to all of this was changing fundamentally how we thought about identity – separating the identifier from the back end, platform identity – capturing all of the events from their phone, from their console or PC, into a single persona – this allows all the data around them to be actioned properly."

## What Are The Key Learning Points And Takeaways?

Video games represent a huge chunk of the entertainment industry and, while revenues from movies and music sales have dwindled, sales in this sector consistently continue to rise. This brings fierce competition between rivals with plentiful resources at their disposal. Big Data analysis gives savvy players a distinct advantage in this game.

Gaming represents the wild frontier of technology – where outlandish and revolutionary ideas can be prototyped and field-tested to an audience of keen, tech-savvy and quick-to-voice-their-opinion consumers. So it's no surprise that Big Data is building its bases in this industry.

With the potential to learn more and more about players, game designers, artists and programmers will be able to create experiences more in tune with what their audiences enjoy. This will lead to more entertaining, immersive and challenging games that will make today's blockbusters like Grand Theft Auto and Call of Duty look like Space Invaders or Pac-Man.

## REFERENCES AND FURTHER READING

1. Taneja, R. (2013) Video games: The biggest big data challenge, http://conferences.oreilly.com/strata/strata2013/public/schedule/detail/ 27603, accessed 5 January 2016.
2. New Zoo (2015) Top 25 games companies by revenues, http://www. newzoo.com/free/rankings/top-25-companies-by-game-revenues/, accessed 5 January 2016.

For more information on how Big Data is used in the videogame industry, see:

http://siliconangle.com/blog/2013/02/28/ea-looks-to-big-data-to-level-up-the-video-game-industry/

## REFERENCES AND FURTHER READING

# 44
# KAGGLE

## *Crowdsourcing Your Data Scientist*

## Background

Kaggle is a crowdsourced data analysis competition platform. Businesses bring their data problems and Kaggle's army of armchair data scientists compete to come up with the best solution.

It's a fascinating idea which has so far seen contestants compete to solve problems ranging from analysing medical records to predicting which patients are likely to need hospitalization, to scanning the deep cosmos for traces of dark matter.

The San Francisco-based company were founded in 2010, inspired by a competition organized by Netflix the previous year. The streaming TV and movie company had challenged the public to come up with better algorithms to predict what their customers would like to watch next, to help them improve their own recommendation engines. Netflix have since gone on to use Kaggle to organize their later competitions.

Chief scientist of Google – one of the many companies which have used Kaggle's services – Hal Varian has described it as: "a way to organize the brainpower of the world's most talented data scientists and make it accessible to organizations of every size".[1]

Anyone can register with Kaggle and enter most of their competitions, competing for prizes of up to $100,000 at the time of writing. Previous competitions such as the Heritage Health Prize in 2012 offered prizes of up to £500,000. Certain competitions, however, are reserved for "masters": site members who have proved their mettle in previous competitions.

## What Problem Is Big Data Helping To Solve?

Companies around the world have acknowledged that there is a serious shortage of trained data scientists. One report by leading analysts Gartner found that over half of the organizations they queried felt their analytics ambitions were restrained by their inability to find suitably skilled employees.[2]

This is due to its being a comparatively new area of IT expertise. Statisticians and business intelligence experts have always been learning the basics, but applying them to the cutting-edge IT infrastructure needed to monitor, capture and analyse truly big, unstructured, messy data requires a relatively new skillset.

## How Is Big Data Used In Practice?

Essentially, Kaggle acts as a middleman: companies and organizations bring their data, set a problem to solve as well as a deadline and offer a prize.

The data is generally simulated, to avoid privacy concerns around the companies passing on confidential information, as well as commercially sensitive data that could fall into the hands of competitors if offered on a public platform.

Instead of offering a cash prize as is normally the case, when Walmart, the world's biggest retailer, came to Kaggle, they offered a job.

Mandar Thakur, senior recruiter for Walmart's Information Systems Organization, tells me: "The supply and demand gap is always there, especially when it comes to emerging technology. So we have found innovative and creative ways to go about finding talent for our data science and analytics teams. We're always looking for top-notch talent who can come in, contribute and catapult us even further."

Walmart's Kaggle competition involved providing a set of historical sales data and marketing events, such as price rollbacks, seasonal offers and clearance sales. Candidates were tasked with producing predictive models showing how the event schedule would affect sales across each of the departments where sales data was available.

Along with crowdsourcing and predictive modelling, gamification is another tool being used here. The human brain is known to respond well to competitions and challenges, particularly when they are incentivized with rewards. As well as money (or employment), the competition structure of Kaggle is designed to allow entrants to showcase their skills and creativity both in the "armchair analyst" community that has evolved within Kaggle and in the wider world.

## What Were The Results?

As a result of the first competition, held in 2014, several people were recruited into Walmart's analytics team, and the competition was held again the following year in the hope of finding more.

One of the winning entrants, Naveen Peddamail, is now employed at the retail giant's Bentonville, Arkansas headquarters as a senior statistical analyst. He tells me: "I already had a job with a consultancy, so was really just browsing Kaggle as a hobby.

"I saw the Walmart challenge and thought I would give it a try. I thought I'd try to do some predictive analytics. After preparing and submitting my model, I ended up among the top entrants and was invited to meet with Walmart's analytics team.

"That's when things really got interesting – when I saw how departments would come to the analytics teams with their problems, and would be able to work through them in 20 or 30 minutes, rather than two or three weeks, as was usually the case, I found it very exciting.

"Everything they were talking about – how to deliver real-time, predictive analytics – working out how to get real insights out of this huge amount of data, that's when I saw the real value in this 'Big Data' that everyone was talking about."

Additionally, Thakur says there were other benefits aside from filling vacancies, for both Walmart and the analytics community at large.

He says: "Kaggle created a buzz around Walmart and our analytics organization. People always knew that Walmart generated a lot of data but the best part was letting them see how we use it strategically."

## What Data Was Used?

For the Walmart competition, entrants were provided with simulated historical sales data from a number of stores, along with dates and details of promotional events, such as sales and public holidays, which it was thought would influence the sales of the item listed.

Other competitions on the site challenge entrants to predict which customers are most likely to respond to direct-mail marketing campaigns, using simulated personal data, identifying physics phenomena using data from CERN's Large Hadron Collider and predicting categories of crime that will be committed in San Francisco, using demographic and historical crime data.

# What Are The Technical Details?

Kaggle pass on raw, simulated datasets from their customers for the "armchair data scientists" on the site to conduct their own analytics. A services layer running on the Unix backbone system allows user-submitted code to be run on their servers, to allow users to submit and demonstrate algorithms entered into competitions. They are planning to extend the capabilities of this system in the near future, as a current job vacancy calls for an engineer to help them transform "from a site for running machine learning competitions to a platform for advanced data science".

# Any Challenges That Had To Be Overcome?

With the growth in popularity of Big Data analysis in business, one thing that has become apparent is that pure number-crunching talent is not always enough to make a great data scientist. Communication ability is also a vital skill. As Thakur put it: "Fundamentally, we need people who are absolute data geeks, people who love data and can slice it, dice it and make it do what they want it to do.

"Having said that, there is one very important aspect which perhaps differentiates a data analyst from other technologists. It exponentially improves their career prospects if they can match this technical data-geek knowledge with great communication and presentation skills. Someone who has this combination of skills can rise to the top very quickly."

To factor this into their recruitment process, the top-performing competition entrants, having proved their skills in raw analytics, were invited for further assessment at the company's headquarters, with the jobs eventually being awarded to those who showed ability in reporting and communications as well as analytical talent.

# What Are The Key Learning Points And Takeaways?

Great data scientists can come from anywhere. They will not always have a formal educational background in statistics, mathematics or computer science, as is generally expected. The analytical mindset can be developed in many areas of life.

Crowdsourcing has great potential for identifying emerging talent. It allows employers to stimulate people who may not have previously thought about a serious career in analytics into taking part, perhaps surprising even themselves with what they are capable of doing with analytics and Big Data.

Gamification provides new ways of engaging with people who potentially can help businesses solve their problems. Fostering a competitive element encourages out-of-the-box thinking as those taking part will strive to make sure their ideas stand out from others.

## REFERENCES AND FURTHER READING

1. Reuters (2015) Kaggle raises $11 million in series a financing led by Index Ventures and Khosla Ventures, http://www.reuters.com/article/idUS58636+03-Nov-2011+BW20111103, accessed 5 January 2016.
2. Rivera, J. and van der Meulen, R. (2015) Gartner Survey Highlights Challenges to Hadoop Adoption, http://www.gartner.com/newsroom/id/3051717, accessed 5 January 2016.

For more insights into the way Walmart used Kaggle, see:

Walmart's 2015 Kaggle contest: https://www.kaggle.com/c/walmart-recruiting-sales-in-stormy-weather

How Walmart is tackling the Big Data skills crisis by Bernard Marr: http://www.smartdatacollective.com/bernardmarr/337820/how-walmart-tackling-big-data-skills-crisis

# 45
# AMAZON

*How Predictive Analytics Are Used To Get A
360-Degree View Of Consumers*

## Background

Amazon long ago outgrew their original business model of an online bookshop. They are now one of the world's largest retailers of physical goods, virtual goods such as ebooks and streaming video and more recently Web services.

Much of this has been built on top of their pioneering use of "recommendation engine" technology – systems designed to predict what we want, when we want it and of course offer us the chance to give them money for it.

With this ethos in mind, Amazon have also moved into being a producer of goods and services, rather than just a retailer. As well as commissioning films and TV shows, they build and market electronics, including tablets, TV boxes and streaming hardware.

Even more recently, they have moved to take on food supermarkets head-on by offering fresh produce and far quicker delivery through their Amazon Now service.

## What Problem Is Big Data Helping To Solve?

Information overload is a very real problem, and retailers have more to lose from it than most of us. Online retailing relies on making as large a number of products or services available as possible, to increase the probability of making sales. Companies like Amazon and Walmart have thrived by adopting an "everything under one roof" supermarket model.

The problem here is that a customer can often feel overwhelmed when presented with a huge range of possible options. Psychologically, worries about suffering from "buyer's remorse" – wasting money by making ill-informed purchasing decisions – can lead to our putting off spending money until we are certain we have done sufficient research. The confusing amount of options may even cause us to change our minds entirely about the fact we need a $2,000 ultraHD television set and decide to go on vacation instead.

It's the same problem that often plagues many projects involving large amounts of information. Customers can become data-rich (with a great many options) but insight-poor – with little idea about what would be the best purchasing decision to meet their needs and desires.

## How Is Big Data Used In Practice?

Essentially, Amazon have used Big Data gathered from customers while they browse the site to build and fine-tune their recommendation engine.

Amazon probably didn't invent the recommendation engine but they introduced it to widespread public use. The theory is that the more they know about you, the more likely they are to be able to predict what you want to buy. Once they've done that, they can streamline the process of persuading you to buy it by cutting out the need for you to search through their catalogue.

Amazon's recommendation engine is based on collaborative filtering. This means that it decides what it thinks you want by working out who you are, then offering you items that people with a similar profile to you have purchased.

Unlike with content-based filtering – as seen, for example, in Netflix's recommendation engine – this means the system does not actually have to know anything about the unstructured data within the products it sells. All it needs is the metadata: the name of the product, how much it costs, who else has bought it and similar information.

Amazon gather data on every one of their over a quarter of a billion customers while they use their services.[1] As well as what you buy, they monitor what you look at, your shipping address to determine demographic data (they can take a good stab at guessing your income level by knowing what neighbourhood you live in) and whether you leave customer reviews and feedback.

They also look at the time of day you are browsing, to determine your habitual behaviours and match your data with others who follow similar patterns.

If you use their streaming services, such as Amazon Prime streaming video or ebook rental, they can also tell how much of your time you devote to watching movies or reading books.

All of this data is used to build up a "360-degree view" of you as an individual customer. Based on this, Amazon can find other people who they think fit into the same precisely refined consumer niche (employed males between 18 and 45, living in a rented house with an income of over $30,000 who enjoy foreign films, for example) and make recommendations based on what they like.

In 2013, Amazon began selling this data to advertisers, to allow them to launch their own Big Data-driven marketing campaigns. This put them in competition with Google and Facebook, which also sell anonymized access to user data to advertisers.

## What Were The Results?

Amazon have grown to become the largest online retailer in the US based on their customer-focused approach to recommendation technology. Last year, they took in nearly $90 billion from worldwide sales.

Revenues for their cloud-based Web services businesses such as Amazon Web Services have grown 81% in the last year, to $1.8 billion.

In addition, Amazon's approach to Big Data-driven shopping and customer services has made them a globally recognized brand.

## What Data Was Used?

Amazon collect data from users as they browse the site – monitoring everything from the time they spend browsing each page to the language used in the user reviews they leave. Additionally, they use external datasets such as census information to establish our demographic details. If you use their mobile apps on your GPS-enabled smartphone or tablet, they can also gather your location data and information about other apps and services you use on your phone. Using Amazon's streaming content services, such as Amazon Prime and Audible, provides them with more detailed information on where, when and how you watch and listen to TV, film and audio.

## What Are The Technical Details?

Amazon's core business is handled in their central data warehouse, which consists of Hewlett-Packard servers running Oracle on Linux, to handle their 187 million unique monthly website visitors, and over two million third-party Amazon Marketplace sellers.

## Any Challenges That Had To Be Overcome?

In the early days, by far the biggest challenge for Amazon and all e-tailers was getting the public to put their faith in taking part in online commercial activity. These days, thanks to enhanced security and legislative pressure (and in spite of ever-increasing incidences of data theft), most of us are no more wary of giving our card details to an online retailer than we are to a bricks 'n' mortar one. Amazon use Netscape Secure Commerce Server systems and SSL to store sensitive information in an encrypted database.

## What Are The Key Learning Points And Takeaways?

Diversity of consumer choice is a great thing, but too much choice and too little guidance can confuse customers and put them off making purchasing decisions.

Big Data recommendation engines simplify the task of predicting what a customer wants, by profiling them and looking at the purchase history of people who fit into similar niches.

The more a business knows about a customer, the better it can sell to them. Developing a 360-degree view of each customer as an individual is the foundation of Big Data-driven marketing and customer service.

Privacy and information security is an absolute priority. One large-scale data breach or theft can destroy consumer confidence in a business overnight.

### REFERENCES AND FURTHER READING

1. Statista (2015) Annual number of worldwide active Amazon customer accounts from 1997 to 2014 (in millions), http://www.statista.com/

statistics/237810/number-of-active-amazon-customer-accounts-world-wide/, accessed 5 January 2016.

For further details on Amazon's use of Big Data, see:

https://datafloq.com/read/amazon-leveraging-big-data/517

http://expandedramblings.com/index.php/amazon-statistics/

Scientific explanation of Amazon's recommendation engine, and collaborative filtering in general, by Greg Linden, Brent Smith, and Jeremy York of Amazon. http://www.scribd.com/doc/14771615/Amazon-Recommendations

# FINAL THOUGHTS

I feel extremely lucky and privileged to work in the field of Big Data, where I am able to help companies and government organizations across all sectors and industries find new and better ways to use data and analytics to deliver real value. My work allows me to learn about new and innovative ways companies apply Big Data.

With this book I wanted to provide a compressive overview of the current state of play in Big Data. However, in such a fast-moving environment, that is difficult. This last week I have worked with a credit card provider who is doing amazing things with big data, analysing millions of transactions in near real time. This would have made another great chapter for this book. Today, I have been in touch with two of the companies featured in this book that have implemented new initiatives and applied new technology to derive even better value from their big data. Next week, I am going to Spain to meet the analytics team at FC Barcelona to explore how Big Data and analytics are used in professional football.

This field is developing so fast that it is impossible to capture everything that is happening. I hope this book has given you a good overview of the things happening right now. It hopefully shows that Big Data is very real and companies are using it every day to improve what they do and how they do it.

The next few years will see companies who ignore Big Data be overtaken by those who don't. I very much believe that any organization without a Big Data strategy and without plans in place to start using Big Data to improve performance will be left behind.

It is impossible to predict the future of Big Data, but I can see the term disappearing (because it will no longer be needed to emphasize a new phenomenon); in fact, I have never liked the term, because it overemphasizes the size of data rather than the variety and what we do with it. I much prefer to talk about SMART Data, as outlined in my previous book *Big Data: Using SMART Big Data, Analytics and Metrics To Make Better Decisions and Improve Performance.*

SMART applications of Big Data start with your strategy in order to identify the areas in which data can make the biggest difference to your performance and decision making. Only once you are clear about the strategic questions Big Data could help you to answer should you start to collect and analyse the data to help you answer those questions and transform your organization. I believe the case studies in this book show how these principles are applied well. However, in practice I see a lot of companies that get lost in the Big Data opportunities and end up hoarding data in the mistaken believe it will, some day, become useful.

My biggest piece of advice would be to start with your strategy and identify the big challenges and areas in which data will make the biggest difference. Only then collect and analyse the data that will help you meet those challenges. Don't fall into the trap of collecting and analysing everything you can and nothing that matters.

In terms of other future developments, I also see huge innovations in related fields, such as the Internet of Things, machine learning and artificial intelligence. These will affect the developments of Big Data and make the phenomenon become even more important.

If I were to look into the crystal ball then I would see an increasing move to real-time analytics where large volumes of data (structured and unstructured) are analysed in almost real time to inform decision making and to feed machine-learning algorithms.

There is no doubt that Big Data will give us many innovations and improvements but it will also challenge us in areas such as data privacy and data protection. The ability to analyse everything we do in the wrong hands can cause unthinkable harm. It will be up to all of us to ensure the right legal frameworks are in place to protect us from the misuse of Big Data.

Overall, Big Data is a fascinating and fast-moving field. I will continue to share my insights and the latest developments. If you would like to keep informed and continue the debate then please connect with me on LinkedIn and Twitter, where I regularly share all my writings. You can find me on LinkedIn under Bernard Marr and on Twitter with the handle: @bernardmarr.

For more information and to get in touch with me, please visit my website at www.ap-institute.com, where you can find lots of relevant articles, white papers, case studies, videos and much more.

# ABOUT THE AUTHOR

**Bernard Marr** is the founder and CEO of the Advanced Performance Institute, an organization that specializes in improving business performance and decision making through the use of data.

Bernard is a best-selling business author, keynote speaker and consultant in big data, analytics and enterprise performance. He is one of the world's most highly respected voices anywhere when it comes to data in business. His leading-edge work with major companies, organizations and governments across the globe makes him a globally acclaimed and award-winning researcher, consultant and teacher.

Bernard is a regular contributor to the World Economic Forum, is acknowledged by the CEO Journal as one of today's leading business brains and by LinkedIn as one of the World's top-five business Influencers of 2015.

His articles and expert comments regularly feature in high-profile publications including *The Times*, *The Financial Times*, *Financial Management*, *Forbes*, the *CFO Magazine*, the *Huffington Post* and the *Wall Street Journal*. Bernard is an avid tweeter and the writer of regular columns for LinkedIn Pulse.

He has written a number of seminal books and hundreds of high-profile reports and articles. This includes the best-sellers *Big Data: Using SMART Big Data, Analytics and Metrics to Make Better Decisions and Improve Performance, Key Business Analytics: The 60+ Business Analysis Tools Every Manager Needs to Know, The Intelligent Company* and *Big Data for Small Business* in the *For Dummies* series.

Bernard has worked with and advised many of the world's best-known organizations, including Accenture, AstraZeneca, Bank of England, Barclays, BP, DHL, Fujitsu, Gartner, HSBC, IBM, Mars, the Ministry of Defence, Microsoft, NATO, Oracle, the Home Office, the NHS, Orange, Tetley, T-Mobile, Toyota, the Royal Air Force, SAP, Shell and the United Nations, among many others.

If you would like to talk to Bernard about any data project you require help with or if you are thinking about running a Big Data event or training course in your organization and need a speaker or trainer, contact him at www.ap-institute.com or via email at: bernard.marr@ap-institute.com.

You can also follow @bernardmarr on Twitter, where he regularly shares his ideas, or connect with him on LinkedIn or Forbes, where he writes regular blogs.

# ACKNOWLEDGEMENTS

I am so grateful to everyone who has helped me get to where I am today. All the great people in the companies I have worked with who put their trust in me to help them and in return give me so much new knowledge and experience. I must also thank everyone who has shared their thinking with me, either in person, in blog posts, books or any other formats. Thank you for generously sharing all the material I absorb every day! I am also lucky enough to personally know many of the key thinkers and thought leaders in the field and I hope you all know how much I value your inputs and our exchanges. At this point I usually start a long list of key people but I always miss some off, so this time I want to resist that and hope your egos will forgive me. You are all amazing!

Finally, I want to thank the team at Wiley for all their support. Taking any book through production is always a challenging process and I really appreciate your input and help.

# INDEX